LEADERS MUST LEAD!

THE PATH TO MASTERY

In a world where there is no such thing as
sustainable competitive advantage...

LEADERS MUST LEAD!

JOHN O. BURDETT

Leaders Must Lead

www.orxestra.com

ISBN 0-9687233-2-2

National Library of Canada Cataloguing

HD57.7.B87 2002   658.4'092 C2002-902874-4

Third Printing

Published by:

Executive Forum, a division of Canada Forum Inc.

Toronto, Canada

Individual and bulk orders can be placed:

In Toronto (416) 925-0866

In North America 1-800-443-6452

info@canadaforum.com

Printed in Canada

"It is not the critic who counts;

not the one who points out how the strong stumbled,

or where the doer of deeds could have done better.

The credit belongs to those in the arena;

who strive valiantly;

who fail and come up short again and again;

who know great enthusiasm and great devotion;

who at the best know in the end

the triumph of high achievement;

and who, at the worst, if they fail,

at least fail while daring greatly,

so that their place shall never be with

those timid souls who

know neither victory nor defeat!"

Theodore Roosevelt

Introduction

We live in turbulent times. The river we stand in is not the river that will carry us forth. To relax is to concede victory. Success is the clearest indicator that failure beckons. If it worked yesterday...reinvent it. Celebrate success by all means, but do so with the sure knowledge that what you are applauding is already redundant. The faster you become, the faster, of necessity, will become those who also harbor a passion to win. One move changes the whole complexion of the game. Yesterday's leaders played checkers. Today's game is three-dimensional chess. The more successful you become, the more certain you can be that others will be forced to attack your queen.

Leadership is at a premium. Even the best enterprises are woefully short of talent. Where did all the leaders go? They didn't go anywhere. What the times demand is leadership of an entirely different order.

Forget about trying to exercise power. Think more about how to gain power by giving it away. Forget about the three-day retreat to develop tomorrow's strategy. It will be out of date before you get back to the office. Drop the notion that people follow you because of your position. You are competing for people's dreams. If someone has a more compelling dream...get out of the way. Forget the lines of responsibility on the organization chart. If you tried to make it work that way you would need twice as many people as you have now. Extinguish the thought that you are in charge. Recognize that leadership is a privilege extended to you by those who choose to work with you. And throw out even the slim belief that *you* have accomplished anything. If you brought focus, created the environment for people to grow and, most important of all, had the good sense to get out of the way, take satisfaction in the knowledge that you were part of a successful team.

Most of all, jettison the notion that leadership is something that can be acquired in a red brick institution or its corporate substitute. Leadership is not a spectator sport. Leadership is about action... it's about change. Leaders learn to lead by leading. That doesn't mean that ideas, thought and reflection aren't essential companions on the journey. Indeed, without new ideas little is possible. As for a new leadership direction: we have no choice…the enemy is at the gate.

No sports team can hold the ultimate prize if their marquee players don't play up to their full potential. In a similar vein, no organization can sustain success if those who wear the mantle of leadership do not provide leadership. Simply put, **Leaders Must Lead**.

Without vibrant and energetic leadership, organizations cannot survive. Millions spent on the finest consulting minds count for naught if the talent to carry out that which is prescribed is lacking. The most elegant structure is a mere bagatelle if inspiration is missing. Even the most elegant systems are redundant without trust. An organization without leadership is an empty shell. It's all about leadership! But, and this is an important but, leaders must lead. Leaders must be given the opportunity to lead, they must be given the space to lead, they must be provided with the tools to lead but, most important of all, those in positions of responsibility must have the inner fiber that *compels* them to lead. Anything less is to strive for mediocrity.

This brings me to a key metaphor introduced in part one of this book: **the Red Queen**. The Red Queen analogy was proposed by evolutionary biologist L. van Valen in 1973, and inspired by a quotation from the character of the Red Queen in Lewis Carroll's *Through the Looking Glass*. "A slow sort of country!" said the Queen. "Now, *here*, you see, it takes all the running you can do, to keep in the same place. If you want to get somewhere else, you must run at least twice as fast as that."

Darwinism is based on the survival of the fittest. The natural conclusion of this argument is that as one species gains competitive advantage over its competitors it captures a larger share of the resources available. Van Valen argues that success in one species leads not to a lasting competitive edge but to improved competition. If the cheetah runs faster, the antelope on which it preys will, of necessity, also learn how to run faster. Thus, progress is always relative and competitive advantage always temporary. In the Queen's words, "it takes all the running you can do to stay in the same place." The "arms race" is often seen as the political equivalent of the "Red Queen Effect." Van Valen also points out that the most aggressive competition is not between common species (e.g. mammals) but between those competing for the same resources. For example, it is often forgotten that the 1918 flu pandemic killed more people than did World War I. Terrible as the recent wars in Africa have been, man's most aggressive competitor is AIDS.

The lessons for business are clear: (1) to gain competitive advantage you have to run twice as fast; (2) any competitive advantage is temporary; and (3) tomorrow's competition is likely to come from a source that is unanticipated. This book describes this overall business environment as a "Red Queen World."

As a practitioner I am interested in what outstanding leaders actually do. What makes them successful? What sort of legacy do they leave? How do they make a difference? If there is one source for the material in the book, it is my clients. During the last decade I have worked in thirty countries, met with literally hundreds of groups, and consulted with dozens of companies. Sometimes consulting means working with the top team, but as often as not the dialogue takes place in workshops that include people from across the organization. The ideas presented also draw from a wide spectrum of industries ranging from high-tech to aluminum, from biotech to packaging, from medical equipment to consulting, from automotive parts to pharmaceuticals, from hospitality to telecoms.

Perhaps most important of all, I have drawn on discussions with leaders whose roles give them an international perspective. I am, as a result, indebted to the many executives who, during an early morning walk, or over a coffee, or a beer, were willing to share their thoughts and talk about the issues that faced them. If writing the book has been a joy, the conversations in a mountain hut in Switzerland, a game park in South Africa, a beachside hotel in Florida, a bar in Helsinki, or as first light falls on the Three Sisters in the Blue Mountains of New South Wales, have been pure privilege.

There is yet one more group that has added significantly to my own learning. Over the past few years I have had the opportunity – on both sides of the Atlantic – to coach a number of senior executives. It is a humbling experience to find oneself as the alter ego with whom a top leader chooses to share his/her concerns, provocative views and blue-sky thinking. Being a good coach entails an openness to being coached. Each meaningful coaching conversation is a shared learning experience.

The book was written with the certain knowledge that time is of the essence to today's leaders. Few have the time to sit down and read even a slimmed-down book from cover to cover. What chances there are amount to forty minutes snatched on the subway and/or in the hour and a half between take-off and oxygen-starved drowsiness on an overnight transatlantic flight. Recognizing that these are the windows of opportunity, each chapter is presented as a stand-alone formulation of ideas, linked to the whole, but having meaning on its own. It is a deliberate invitation to browse and dip.

> *Book One: Leadership of the Organization.* Chapter One looks at strategy, speed, and simplicity. Not strategic planning of which a great deal is written, but *strategy implementation.* A good many leaders can develop a strategy. It's making it happen that

is the difference that makes a difference. Speed and simplicity are natural and essential elements of implementing strategy. Chapter Two explores the challenge of building common ground: connectability, convergence and creative collaboration. Chapter Three looks at the relationship between learning and change.

Book Two: Leadership of Others. It's tough to argue with the statement, "leadership is about followship." The best way to measure a leader's effectiveness is to find out how successful those who work for him/her are. Are they growing? Can they act independently? Are they willing to take risk? Do they stand up for what they and the organization believe in? Are they willing to commit everything when the opportunity demands it? The challenge: followship doesn't just happen. It is something leaders work at every day. Book Two focuses on four of the critical building blocks of followship: leadership style (Chapter Four); storytelling (Chapter Five); talent acquisition (Chapter Six); and executive coaching (Chapter Seven).

Book Three: Leadership of Self. There is a valid argument that says leadership of self is the foundation around which every other aspect of leadership is built. Leadership of self comes at the end of the book, not because the earlier statement is incorrect, but because Book Three draws on the insight, language and awareness found in Books One and Two. If *Leaders Must Lead!* is, in any way, a journey of discovery, leadership of self is where the various threads are woven into a single tapestry. Accordingly, Chapter Eight takes a deeper look at what is meant by leadership of self. Chapter Nine is described by its title…It's all about trust. And the final chapter, Chapter Ten, poses fundamental questions about personal mastery.

Finally, *Leaders Must Lead!* was written as a natural companion to an earlier book, *New Role, New Reality* (2000). Nominated as Book of the Year by the US Society of Human Resource Management, the earlier publication deals with the challenge of moving into a new role. *Leaders Must Lead!* is aimed at the successful leader seeking to move to the next level of performance.

Contents

Book One

Leadership of the

Organization

Chapter one

Competing in a Red Queen World:
making strategy happen

Book One
Leadership of the Organization

A new business model?

To an army of wired warriors it was hip…it was sexy. It was wild. It was free. It was cool. Indeed, even after the dust from the dot-com collapse has settled, there is still reference to the "new economy."

Fueled by all the exuberance and passions of the California Gold Rush, it was an entrepreneurial rebellion that, so we were persuaded, defined our age. The philosophical underpinning of this so-called "new era": the apparent belief that in panning for golden eyeballs in cyberspace, growth and momentum take precedence over profitability; mind share is more important than market share; and that hits and stickiness, not cash flow, defined success. Its flaw? It contained within it a perverse logic: if you lose money on every item sold…then, heck, sell more!

The more some things change, the more others stay the same! This is as true in the world of finance as anywhere else for, of course – as many dot-com organizations discovered to their cost – there is no "new" economy. The rules of the old economy work just fine, thank you. Businesses, new or old, live by one undeniable and unbending rule: if you spend more money than you make, you go broke. Simple!

That being said, it is impossible to ignore the fact that there is a new business model. Same economy…new model! It is a way to operate that is embodied in a world without borders:

- Where technology redefines the meaning of community;
- Where the Internet changes dramatically the scope, nature and value of business processes;
- Where giving product away is a viable business strategy (talk to someone in the music industry);

- Where the service provider has real-time access to the customer, regardless of their geographic location;

- Where the stories that people share about the product or service create more lasting value (equity) than do the images and symbolic messages given birth in an advertising studio;

- Where tomorrow's competition is likely to come from a source that is virtually impossible to predict.

More than anything else, however, it's a world where innovation rules and speed is king. When the rules of the game change – which they inevitably must, regardless of the industry – speed of action determines who thrives and who dies.

The need to do things, not just better, but faster, is no small thing. The capacity to act fast changes irrevocably what it takes to be a leader. Gone forever is the notion that exhaustive research and in-depth analysis are the keys to effective decision-making. Welcome to a context where being 70% right is a luxury. Welcome to a world where every act of micro-management robs the organization of its vitality. Welcome to a marketplace where knowing how to fail fast is an imperative. And welcome to an environment where game playing, political expediency, a need for rules, and adherence to past practice are to an organization what speed bumps are to a noisy kid on a skateboard.

Don't be seduced into believing that, because the dot-coms got into trouble, speed is exclusively a feature of the Internet puppies. To survive, even the old dogs must learn new ways to bark! The challenge: not merely how to think "fast," but something far more difficult, how to **act** fast. Part of the answer lies in examining how strategy has evolved. Strategy has always been a weathervane for the thinking of the day.

Strategic planning: dead but won't lie down

The link between leadership and strategy is hardly new. Anticipating where the caribou would be, timing the move to the high pasture, marshalling resources to ward off attack were all strategic issues that dominated life for thousands of years. In similar fashion, since the time of Alexander the Great, strategy and military command have been synonymous; something that business leaders were quick to emulate.

It wasn't until the 1960s, however, that business strategy started to move into high gear. The shift: leaders in the sixties grabbed hold of planning, budgeting and the newly-minted management by objectives (MBO) as the way to forge a common direction. The theme: ever-more *Control*.

The seventies gave birth to strategic business units, portfolio planning, and the separation of operational know-how and corporate intelligence. The long view became the prerogative of the corporate strategic planning team. In dogs, cash cows, stars and problem children were to be found the rationale for allocating scarce resources. Portfolio planning, it was suggested, allowed the CEO to better analyze performance and thus allocate resources more effectively *across* all of the business. In the late seventies a perceived need for even greater attention to detail resulted in like business units being organized into sectors. The theme: ***Give me the numbers***.

In the eighties the wheels fell off "the central planning train" and line managers were back in charge. The consulting industry was quick to promote its expertise. The famed "strategic retreat" was in. The theme: ***Consultants know best***. What was needed was simplicity. What the consulting industry had a vested interest in delivering was a cornucopia of approaches and techniques. The dilemma: after punching the operator's ticket, the conductor got off the train. The good news: culture, vision, and the need for alignment around the organization's core values found their way onto the corporate radar screen.

The nineteen-nineties introduced rejection of "the plan" altogether. In a world that was changing at the speed of thought, "the formulated strategy" was often redundant before the ink was dry. The reality: if you make a decision to cross the street based on yesterday's traffic flow, don't be surprised if you get hit by a truck. Napoleon was proven to be prophetically right when he said, "Strategy is forgotten when the first cannon is fired." The answer: push more and more strategic decisions to those who actually deal with the customer; make agility a key priority; and *build organizational capability* to support eight, ten, even twenty, well thought-through future scenarios. The theme: ***Forget "the plan," find the patterns***.

The arrival of the twenty-first century, and with it the collapse of the dot-com companies, merely emphasized the futility of assuming past events are a harbinger of things to come.

In a "scenaric" approach, "the plan" is replaced by a series of scenarios. Each is a well-crafted story rich in language and imagery, each an attempt to capture the fears, anxiety, possibilities and pathways that lead to an uncertain future.

Scenario thinking is significantly aided when those involved come from different backgrounds, read widely, and are comfortable asking "dumb" questions. The scenarios should be seen not as stand-alone projections but as a series of sub-plots in the same play. Only in this way can the underlying patterns and the linkage between critical events be discerned. The potential for breakthrough thinking lies in the collective starburst, not the individual vapor trails.

A well-narrated scenario will challenge today's mindsets. It is a shrill warning to those lulled into a false sense of security, a wakeup call to those wrapped in the security of events past, and a rallying cry to those with the courage to take the lead.

Framed by the organization's mission (raison d'être), scenarios live and breathe when real-time software gives the opportunity for new information to be added, "what if" questions answered, and input from external knowledge experts factored in.

When everything is stripped away, strategic thinking is prompted by three simple questions. The first: *"What is the worst thing the competition could do?"* The leadership response: act while the competition is still thinking about it. This is what Norman Hunter, the legendary English soccer player, referred to as "retaliating first." Norman, it need not be added, took no prisoners! The second and third questions: *"If we weren't in this business would we get into it? If we didn't have this product or service would we create it?"*

The inevitable outcome of a heightened uncertainty was the decline of nice, normal, linear, rational, strategic planning in favor of its crazy, irreverent second cousin, strategic thinking. Leaders were learning what tennis, ice hockey, and soccer greats have always known…the faster the game, the more winning becomes the art of anticipation. What we carried into this century is that left-brain logic has to be joined – and even overruled – by right brain intuition. Here again, however, one is reminded of the question Corsica's most famous son asked when determining if one of his officers was fit for command, "Is he lucky?"

A Red Queen World

"A slow sort of country!" said the Queen. "Now, *here*, you see, it takes all the running you can do, to keep in the same place. If you want to get somewhere else, you must run at least twice as fast as that." These lines from Lewis Carroll's *Through the Looking Glass* inspired the evolutionary biologist L. van Valen, in 1973, to coin a term for the temporary nature of competitive advantage… "The Red Queen Effect." The Red Queen Effect concludes that any evolutionary system needs to develop just to maintain its fitness relative to its competitors. Moreover, the greater the competitive advantage any single species gains, the more likely those competing for the same resources are to improve their own design. Simply put: the more successful you become the harder you have to run. In a world where continuous reinvention becomes the norm, running fast amounts to little more than staying put. Organizations that want to get somewhere else have to run twice as fast as that.

In a world where continuous reinvention becomes the norm, running fast amounts to little more than staying put.

Be prepared to jettison your most valued cargo. Be willing to let go of that which you most prize. Embrace constructive destruction as a way of life. Speed demands not new ways to act, but new ways to think. It is not merely a matter of putting Drucker on steroids. There is no "speed" elixir…no Viagra-like potion for leadership vagrants. This is not to imply speed for the sake of speed. There is nothing smart in a frenetic, bone-shaking ride to self-destruction. Speed delivers a simple reality: if you want the best seats, you had better be at the theatre before anyone else.

Speed is an outcome of "systems thinking." Change one thing and everything else changes. A focus on a single performance characteristic to the exclusion of any other severely limits what is possible. Pushing more power into the engine of the family car without considering the resulting stress on every other component is to guarantee a breakdown.

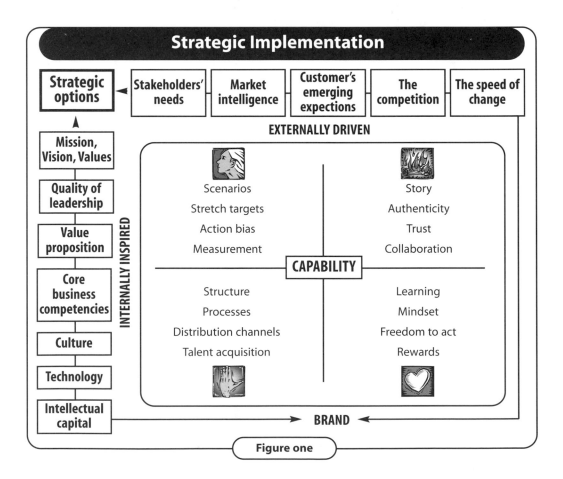

Figure one

Speed is not an end in itself. Speed that does not create value is meaningless. Speed means learning faster than the competition. Speed means responding to opportunity before anyone else does. Speed means being able to turn on a dime when a killer application enters the market. When all is said and done, however, speed is all about how quickly strategy **is implemented**. The Achilles heel of modern leadership isn't the ability to create a new strategy. Most organizations are knee deep in strategy. Where leaders struggle is in making the strategy work and doing so fast enough. Strategic implementation is ultimately dependent upon two key organizational characteristics. The first: the firm must be quick to understand and, where necessary, rechart its **strategic options.** The second: the firm must have the **capability** to deliver the option(s) agreed on.

The organization's strategic options are a product of (1) external forces and (2) its access to leading edge processes and people. (*See Figure one.*) **Capability is what the organization can actually deliver. Building capability is the key to strategic implementation.**

Capability is brought to life in the organization's brand. "Brand" is far more than a label. It's where all of the threads come together. It is a means to capture the organization's identity. It states to the world in general, "This is who we are!" It's a story that is constantly being told through imagery, symbolism, language, and – in a successful business – action. It is a *specific* promise to the customer. **It is also an *implied* promise to every employee!** No organization can deliver in the market place that which it does not practice inside the business. Customers are far too smart to be seduced into believing in a promise employees know to be "dishonest." (See Chapter Nine, "It's all about trust.")

Capability is not a "Let's get to it tomorrow" issue. In a Red Queen World, it's something that leaders must work at *every* day. In an era past, this work would have been dominated by an approach best described as "head and hand." Unfortunately, strategy, goals, and a better sense of tomorrow, on their own, do not equip us for an uncertain future. Driving down cost may prepare the ground but it does not contain within it the seeds of greatness. Even that clarion call of many a troubled organization, "Let's reorganize," has run its course. And although technology lies at the center of the modern business, without the magic of commitment and meaning it amounts to little more than a black box that no one wants to open. The head and hand are imperative, but on their own they are not leadership. Head and hand "leaders" create momentum, but they do not sustain. This is not to decry the value of the head and hand. Without them we are a solution looking for a problem. Without them we are a motivated worker looking for both a hammer and a nail. Leadership is about balance. Leadership is to deliver "the what" (head), "the how" (hand), "the why" (heart), and "who gains" (spirit). Leaders who leave a legacy, organizations with speed enough to wear the Queen's colors, are those that *continuously* build and, when demanded, *reinvent capability* that addresses the head, involves the hand, engages the heart and enriches the spirit.

Capability of the head?

On June 29th, 1863 John Buford rode to the top of a hill from which the ridges of the Blue Mountains of Virginia were plainly visible. Buford was in command of two brigades of cavalry. His orders were to scout the country ahead of the Union army that lay a full day to the rear. He was at Gettysburg. The decision he took, on what was later named Cemetery Hill, was to win a battle, give hope to a nation, and change the world forever.

What he saw before him was a Confederate army that was already forming up in force. He also recognized something else: the hill on which he stood and the wall that ran along one side were the keys to the battle that was about to take place. Without orders and with only 2,500 men, he dug in.

Outnumbered and outgunned, Buford's men hung on to that high ground. Facing him was Harry Heth, one of the South's most determined generals. Time after time the men from south of the Mason-Dixon threw everything they had at Buford's dismounted cavalry… but the line held…. and continued to hold. Buford lived, but within six months was struck down by typhoid. He was made a Major General on his deathbed.

Holding Cemetery Hill was the key to Gettysburg, and Gettysburg was the key to the North's victory in the Civil War. After Gettysberg, the South would never again come close to winning the war.

Capability that draws on the head is about setting out the potential options; agreeing on stretch goals; building partnerships with those who add unique capability; and continuously working at constructive deconstruction. Leaders know the head isn't engaged when the CEO's vision lacks energy; there is no clear winning value proposition; there is disagreement over priorities; there is a surfeit of projects; leaders are confused about their role; what gets measured is misaligned with the customers' emerging needs; front-line employees don't know and/or don't understand the organization's financial results; and the performance management process rewards *yesterday's* competencies.

You can get ready, you can get down, you can get lucky and you can get lost, but you can't get simple! Simplicity isn't something you plan for. Simplicity is a state of mind.

No experienced leader would argue with the belief that an organization lacking a vibrant and engaging vision is missing a key piece of the puzzle. The need to define roles and agree on stretch objectives goes without saying. Linking financial consequences to the performance outcome makes eminent sense. What Buford's courage adds is that strategy, plans, intelligence and knowledge of the enemy – important though they may be – are for naught if the commander in the field doesn't know when to act. Strategic implementation succeeds or falls on this simple premise.

Initiative lies partly in personality and is somewhat the result of a strong sense of self-worth. It is impossible to build high self-esteem without taking risk. That being said, taking risk is, in part, about *knowing that you can take risk*. No responsible astronaut ventures from the shuttle without being tethered, albeit with a single cable, to the mother ship. Breaking, and/or making forays into the white space that exists outside of the prescribed role is only possible if the individual doing so knows that creating value carries precedence over playing it safe. The Gordian thread that allows risk to flourish is constructed out of the freedom to act that the mission, vision, values, and leadership competencies provide. The tensile strength of that thread is, in turn, determined by how the CEO and his/her team respond to constructive failure.

Initiative demands simplicity. You can get ready, you can get down, you can get lucky and you can get lost, but you can't get simple! Simplicity isn't something you plan for. Simplicity is a state of mind. Organizations are starting to operate "simply" when the consultants the organization uses can all go to lunch in the same taxicab; when the CIO speaks a language that the rest of the organization can understand; when e-mails go only to those who need to see them; when reports and assessments can be read in minutes; when the corporate office is small enough for everyone to know the name of the Treasurer's dog; and when, even in the largest enterprise, the organization chart shows no more than four levels between the CEO and the front-line.

Ross Perot was the author of perhaps the best description of simplicity. Right after the organization he had built from scratch (EDS) was taken over by General Motors, he was asked what he thought of the new parent. "If someone at EDS finds a snake, we kill it," he said. "If someone at General Motors finds a snake, first they form a snake committee, then they go out and hire a snake consultant to help them study the snake problem." Simplicity is to kill the snake!

To implement successfully is to set the stage and then assume that the unexpected will happen. Speed lies in the art of delegation, giving people the space to act, but being around if things go amiss. Not to be simple is to be complex. Complexity smothers initiative and destroys responsiveness. "Pass me that stick, I see another damn snake!"

Capability of the hand?

Implementation, as described by the hand, is expressed in the organization design, structure, process, technology, systems, and the distribution channels needed to create value. Capability of the hand builds the track on which the express train will run. Implementation problems that come to the fore when the hand is not fully represented can be seen in technology that takes far too long to implement; high levels of customer complaints; problems getting new products to market; difficulty of competing with new entrants to the market place on price; slow moving inventory; working capital that is too high; and, recruitment practices that either deliver a poor batting average or fail to integrate new leaders.

It was June 18th, 1815. The place: Waterloo. The Prussians were on their way to reinforce the 67,000 British troops. Blücher, the "Iron Prussian," had command of 117,000 men. Were he to reinforce Wellington, Napoleon's force of 72,000 would be overwhelmed.

Napoleon knew he had to attack. If he could force Wellington's center before the Prussians arrived, the day would be won. In reserve he had Marshall Ney and the French cavalry.

Headed by Ney himself, forty squadrons of cavalry crashed down on the British line. The roar of grapeshot filled the air. The field was littered with the mangled dead, men and horses. Deadly though their rate of fire was, the British could not stop the irresistible French attack. The British line was overrun. The guns had to be abandoned. Ney had time to disable the British guns. Except... the French had forgotten to bring the headless nails needed to spike the guns. Napoleon lost Europe for want of a bag of nails.

Speed of decision-making does not mean that attention to detail on those issues where it really matters is forgotten. Doing things right the first time is the fastest way to perform. Keeping existing customers is far less onerous that having to build new relationships. Anticipating both problem and opportunity is as much a part of creating an agile response, as it is the behavior in the moment. Building capability of the hand is to know where and when the detail is demanded. To be fast, but to arrive without the nails, is still to lose the battle.

Regardless of the product or service, the "hand" will always fumble if the basic design of the organization is unsound. Design, organizational or otherwise, is ultimately about fitness for purpose...a table, no matter how elegant, is poorly designed if it is unstable. Data, information and knowledge share many of the properties of water: they flow along the easiest path. Meanwhile, information technology has dramatically increased the number of channels and routes available. The problem: when the newly created and easily accessible pathways are in conflict with the formal organization structure, confusion is the inevitable consequence. Structure that distorts, disrupts and/or redirects how people would ideally choose to communicate, not only makes it far less likely that the elephant will dance, but worse, makes it really, really, mad.

The word "structure" – as opposed to "structures" – implies that a successful business is organized around one unifying principle of organization design. The evidence suggests otherwise. If the business has its operations in a third world country; has outsourced its information technology function; has its core competency tied to a relatively small group of knowledge workers; has formed a strategic alliance with at least one of its competitors; and/or has different relationships with different suppliers…a single way to organize makes absolutely no sense. Only a zookeeper in need of medication would put a moose and a tiger in the same enclosure. The outcome: today's leader, regardless of the size of the operation, must develop the behavioral bandwidth needed to succeed in a range of structures. (See Chapter Four.)

As with organization design, finding talent is a priority that cuts across every organization. Business success cannot exist without excellence in talent acquisition. There are $50 million executives (in terms of the size of company he or she can run), $500 million executives, $5 billion executives and $50 billion executives. Hiring a $500 million executive into a $5 billion company is tantamount to assuming that a candidate whose best trick is to juggle three plates will suddenly be capable of keeping thirty in the air.

So it is with speed. There are those executives whose very DNA includes the "speed gene." Others have the capacity to act, but lack the judgement, maturity and experience needed to make sound decisions. Failure to include speed of thought and action as central to the hire decision is to make a "blind" wager that the newly minted executive can find another gear when needed. Of course, speed without stamina isn't much of a bet either.

Capability of the heart?

Leaders who don't engage the heart are attempting to implement strategy while leaving their most important capability on the sidelines. When the heart is missing, much of the collective energy and vitality needed to drive performance excellence gets channeled into disruptive actions that metaphorically scream at the organization's leadership…we're here and we matter!

The deepest learning is a form of personal kaisen… pushing oneself to the very precipice of failure, finding out what isn't working, fixing it, and then pushing on again.

Capability that doesn't tap into the heart is apparent in unacceptable levels of absenteeism, high turnover, micro-management, defensiveness in the face of change, few employee suggestions, poor image in the job market… and with it, difficulty in attracting talent. Lack of heart can be seen in too many grievances, inter-union rivalry, an adherence to restrictive practices, rivalry between key leaders, and "tell and sell" learning approaches.

The heart is missing when employees find out what's happening in the organization through the press, there is little interest from front-line employees in the financial results, and there are constant demands for higher wages/compensation. Leaders are not engaging the heart when the behavior of key leaders is misaligned with the organization's values, there is a presumption from those orchestrating change that employees resist change, "top gun" rather than team selling predominates, and those who could make a difference choose to sit on the fence.

How quickly people learn dictates how fast the organization can act. Sharing best practice, turning know-how into knowledge, skills in collaboration, teamwork, building communities of practice, the opportunity for reflection, coaching, feedback, mentoring, and the quality of the questions asked, all combine to generate the opportunity for people to learn. That does not mean that they will learn. Learning is anchored in the context. Learning flourishes in a *power to* culture. It is strangled when *power over* leadership dominates.

In 1997 Tiger Woods was the PGA Masters champion, winning by a record twelve strokes. He was acclaimed at the tender age of twenty "the world's greatest golfer" and yet, within weeks, he overhauled his swing and set out to totally reinvent his golf game. In the next nineteen months he won only one tournament. The following year (1999) he won ten of fourteen events and had eight PGA Tour victories. When he achieved victory in the British Open in June 2000 he became the youngest, and only one of four golfers, to have won all four of professional golf's major tournaments. The following year he became the only golfer in history to hold all four at the same time, in what became known as "the Wood's Slam." Tiger, who in 1997 was a champion amongst champions, had set himself the target of being not just the world's best golfer, but *the best ever*. In redefining the limits of his own potential he portrayed what learning in a competitive world is all about.

Learning isn't about knowing, it's about change. Learning is rooted in action. It's not just about wanting to win…it's about winning! Learning at the edge is an act of audacity. It's about setting "impossible" goals and then finding ways to make them a reality. Learning, and especially learning that is in concert with doing things ever faster, is never a comfortable experience. And it's certainly not about people sitting in a room being told what is expected of them. The richest learning takes place at the emotional edge. It is enacted in that narrow ribbon of turbulence that separates excitement from fear. The deepest learning is a form of personal *kaisen*… pushing oneself to the very precipice of failure, finding out what isn't working, fixing it, and then pushing on again. Leaders who lack a passion for learning had better get used to hearing a cry from those who do… "Get out of the way!"

To touch people's hearts is to involve them in the decisions that impact their lives, to keep them informed beyond what they need to know and provide an answer to the ever-present question, "What's in it for me?"

In 1899 Charles H. Duell, Commissioner of the US Office of Patents said, "Everything that can be invented has been invented." In speaking about the then-modern airplane Marechal Ferdinand Foch, Professor of Strategy, Ecole Supérieure de Guerre said, "Airplanes are interesting toys but have no military value." It is claimed that in 1949 Thomas Watson, the chairman of IBM said, "I think there is a world market for maybe five computers." Decca Records, after listening to the Beatles in 1962 told their agent, "We don't like their sound and groups with guitars are on the way out." Ken Olson, the founder of Digital Equipment, once said, "There is no reason anyone would want a computer in their home." After writing a report on reliable overnight delivery Fred Smith, who went on to create Federal Express, was told by his Yale Professor, "The concept is interesting and well-formed, but in order to get more than a 'C,' the idea must be feasible." Even Bill Gates has been guilty of being trapped by his own mindset. In 1981 he commented, "640K ought to be enough for anybody."

Without the tools and capability to work at the level of mindset, yesterday's solution is destined to be tomorrow's response. Without the capacity to impact the way employees think, today's speed of response represents the outer limit of the organization's capabilities. Without the capacity to impact people emotionally, leadership amounts to little more than a control mechanism. To bring about change is to touch people's hearts.

Buying a car, changing jobs, the sort of things we do outside of work, buying a house and our response to new opportunity are dominated not by logic but by emotion. Logic kicks in to justify the emotional choice we have already made. Our decisions are controlled by the mammalian (emotional) part of our brain.

Addressing mindsets is only possible if the leader impacts the individual at an emotional level; if he/she touches people's hearts. To touch people's hearts is to involve them in the decisions that impact their lives, to keep them informed beyond what they need to know and provide an answer to the ever-present question, "What's in it for me?" To touch people's hearts is to pose new questions, encourage curiosity and provide the tools of growth. To touch people's hearts is to change the rhythm of play, create new language and encourage storytelling as a critical leadership skill. To touch people's hearts is to reward a willingness to take risk. To touch people's hearts is to align the values that drive the organization forward with the emotional needs of those who work there. To touch people's hearts is to mentor, coach and give honest feedback. To touch people's hearts is to listen. Above all…to listen.

Capability of the spirit?

There is a story about a man who went to heaven and, because he was first in line that day, was told by Saint Peter that he could meet anyone in heaven he wanted. After a pause the man said, "My spirit. That's who I'd like to meet, my spirit." After hailing a passing chariot, Saint Peter bid the new arrival farewell and told the driver, "Be an absolute angel and drop this man off at his spirit." Well, all came to pass as Saint Peter had promised, and the man was duly introduced to his spirit. "I'm angry at you," the man said. "Why are you angry at me?" said his spirit. "Well," the man replied, "when I was successful there were always two sets of footprints in the sand. On the other hand, when I was struggling, when defeat looked me in the face, when disappointment and failure lay to hand, there was only one set." After a pause that seemed to last for an eternity (this is heaven after all), the man's spirit replied, "What you don't understand is that the single set of footprints was mine. It was me who was carrying you!"

Spirit is what carries us all! Spirit gives hope to the oppressed. Spirit sustains when the future looks bleak. Spirit freed India from its colonial yoke. Spirit, as embodied by Nelson Mandela, is the salve that has started to heal the wounds of apartheid. Spirit is all that many of those caught up in the violence of poverty have left, for spirit is the last thing to wither. And spirit is the flame of creativity within each of us that burns bright the moment it is given oxygen.

Spirit is what makes someone pick up the phone and share, unsolicited, an idea that will make someone else in the organization successful. Spirit turns impossible deadlines into successful outcomes. Spirit is the quality that transforms a disparate group of individuals into a team. Spirit is the intangible in culture and an ever-present force in innovation. Without spirit, strategic implementation is something that happens only when the wind is light, the weather is fair and those involved have to travel no further than the immediate horizon.

Spirit is rooted in authenticity and apparent in openness and honesty. Spirit is created when employees are occupied by work that provides meaning…where the value created is shared with others in the wider community. Spirit is found in the reality that people who don't respect the environment are unlikely to respect each other.

Spirit is truth. Leaders who say one thing and do something different, communication that is slanted to benefit the sender, leadership founded in ego gratification, and an unfair distribution of wealth, all these destroy the spirit.

Organizational capability that does not tap into the spirit is evident in the backbiting and multiple agendas that are characteristic of many so-called "teams." Lack of spirit is apparent when leaders don't find the time to listen to those who buy the organization's product or service. Lack of spirit is found in stories that give new life to yesterday's problems. Lack of spirit is found in the cynicism that greets change initiatives, and the entrenched position of employee representatives. Lack of spirit drives the migratory habits of technology workers and the arrogance of subject experts. Spirit is the nutrient of an organization. Spirit is the air that flows beneath the wings of speed. Without it, even the best-laid strategy cannot take flight.

Despite the deforestation of the whole Amazon region, the Yanomami tribes still retain a precious foothold in Brazil's interior. Although these noble people offer us much, it is unlikely that others will emulate their unique approach to conflict resolution. Male members solve disputes by taking turns smashing a thick pole, taken from the roof of the doughnut-shaped communal dwelling (Yano), across each other's heads. The concussed and bloodied one left standing is deemed to be in the right. By comparison, the parties to a dispute in the Inuit communities of Baffin Island solve their problems by telling each other humorous stories, the one who laughs first being in the wrong. What we are describing here is culture, for it is culture that sets out the social norms for how people behave. Culture is spirit in action.

Culture is never static. It can be transformed with the speed and force of an avalanche – as witnessed in Hungary and Poland following the fall of the Berlin Wall – or it can move with the alacrity of an Alaskan glacier. It took the Catholic Church three centuries to admit that Galileo was right. It was the rejection of scientific thought that resulted in the economic fruits of the Renaissance being gathered, not by the Catholics of Italy and southern Europe, but by the Protestants in Holland and England, a shift of power that is still evident in the cast of today's multi-national corporate giants.

Few words are bandied about with such passion but are so misunderstood as the term "culture." For the pragmatist, culture is merely how things happen around here. For the businessperson, values come to the fore. For the organization development specialist, leadership competencies loom large in any understanding. Anthropologists look to language, story, history, myth, symbolism, the distribution of power and how people learn. Others suggest that what gets measured and thus rewarded is the key to unlocking culture. All of the issues identified say something about culture. Arguably each, like the facet of a diamond, is a window to the whole. In being introduced to one we are shaking hands with them all.

The paradox of culture is that each of us is acutely aware of that happening around us. Given that some of us are better at it than others, our extraordinary ability to understand the subtleties and nuances of the world we inhabit is what makes thriving and surviving in a complex world even possible. The dilemma: deep-rooted, intuitive understanding is not the same as being able to surface and articulate those nuances. The challenge: to make culture live.

The clear message from organizations that have a track record of success of strategic implementation is that culture must move out of the realm of conjecture and implied need to become a "hard" dimension of how leadership is enacted. Rigor, vitality, measurement and focus are as critical to the thinking around culture as they are to the organization's physical resources.

Tomorrow's game will be faster

A high percentage of all top leaders fail. The research on organizational change initiatives suggests that 80% plus fall far short of delivering on the goals set. The hit rate on mergers and acquisitions is not the stuff of legend. And we all know the dot-com story. In a world of uncertainty all that can be said with certainty is that there is a high probability that any plan will be wrong.

Leaders fail, not because of the viability of planning tools, but because they don't know how to fix what isn't working. They fail because even when they chart the right course they don't know how to get there. They fail because the crew they lead doesn't know how to change course. They fail because the reaction time of the leaders they direct is too slow. Strategic implementation clearly isn't easy. And it's certainly not a mechanistic process. Those who hold the high ground, those who deliver faster than the competition, build not a strategy but strategic capability. It is a capability that encompasses the head and the hand. Managers are content to stop there. Leaders go deeper. They are driven to also build capability of the heart and the spirit.

The rhythm of business has changed. It will continue to change. Scarier still, today's pace will seem pedestrian five years from now. Speed is an imperative, implementation the stuff of champions. The passport that carries our name is a global, broadband, Red Queen, cyberspace, cultural chip that downloads multiple-track challenges in real-time. It is an invitation to the future that comes stamped with a bold warning…tomorrow's game will be faster.

We cannot, of course, leave without paying respects to our Red Monarch. Her royal edict: "The winners will not be the biggest, those with the best technology, the longest reach, or the organization with the most valuable brand. It will not even be those who fight the hardest. Those who come up trumps will be those who build capability to *become*… the Red Queen."

What to do differently on Monday

1. Set out a chair for the Red Queen. Bring your team together and explore the scenarios that define an uncertain future. Ask, "what's the worst thing the competition could do?" As you read this someone else is literally reinventing your business. Retaliate first.

2. Focus on the value proposition that your organization stands behind. Does it truly differentiate the organization's product and/or services? Does it answer the question: "We already work with several excellent providers, why should we use you?" Build a winning value proposition as a business imperative. Make how to reinvent value for tomorrow's customer an ongoing process.

3. Critically examine the message contained in the brand. It may be a successful emotional hook in the marketplace, but does it live and thrive inside the organization? Develop and deliver the actions needed to make "the brand" how people inside the organization think and act. (See also Chapter Three.)

4. Bring the team together and build on the belief… if we don't burn we don't earn. Seek ways to strip out those elements of how the business operates that put a brake on speed. As a place to start look at the structure, the rule book, approval procedures, how decisions are made, time to market, the role of the center, the markets served, outsourcing of non-core functions and the extent to which front-line employees have the freedom to act.

5. Taken overall, organizations fail not because they lack strategic thinking but because they fail to implement the strategy that has been agreed upon. Implementation, in turn, is about building capability. Capability must encompass the head, the hand, the heart and the spirit. Revisit the Chapter and think about your area of influence. Determine where you need to build capability. Act first on those things you can do that will build the heart and spirit aspects of capability.

Chapter two

Delivering on the promise of collaborative networks

Book One
Leadership of the Organization

In a Red Queen World the charismatic, stand-alone, get-out-of-my-way-I'm-in-charge leader is a fading actor whose time has passed. The Lone Ranger has ridden into his last sunset; Tonto can continue eating prunes in a retirement home; and only a time machine would enable the equine member of our triad to hear one last time those hearty words... "Hi Yo Silver!"

Working in teams is more vital than ever. That does not mean it is the teamwork of yesterday. Teamwork in the traditional sense is dead. Sports as a metaphor to describe team excellence has lost its meaning. And forget any notion of "team" in the singular. Today's leader finds him/herself in an often-bewildering array of different teams. Technology, strategic alliance, partnership, outsourcing and the emerging innovative business models, all redefine how people work together. Moreover, in that language creates imagery and imagery shapes behavior, language is no small thing. The result: leaders have reached out for rich and descriptive terms such as "the network organization," "creative collaboration," "convergence," "connectability," and "co-creation" to describe the nature of these new working relationships.

The need for collaborative networks is something that every business leader can relate to. The operation in Syracuse has discovered how to deal with a critical quality problem, but for some reason no one else in the organization knows about it. Key account selling works in Australia but the African business is struggling on exactly the same topic and guess what, they don't talk! A major UK division has created an e-learning platform but its organizational counterpart in France feels compelled to do their own thing. Executive succession is deemed to be a problem when viewed from the center, but doesn't appear to concern the local human resource executive. New ideas and creativity thrive in one plant but are stifled in its sister plant up the road. The same customer is served in several countries, but no common database is available. What is at stake is an appalling waste of capital in general, and human capital in particular. Put more colorfully, the resulting frustration is the organizational equivalent of regularly adding sand to the gas tank of a very expensive automobile.

The dilemma: few organizations deliver on the promise of collaboration. Like much in life, there is no simple reason, nor for that matter an easy remedy. And the way forward? Collaboration is not an intellectual or academic issue. More thinking and/or study aren't the answer. You can't teach collaboration. What's more, people don't need to learn what they already know. The path forward lies with simply getting on with it. The pragmatism implied is underscored by the following questions.

1. Does the culture reinforce collaboration?

The discussions around leadership and change that do not include the term "culture" are few and far between. In a sense that's the good news. The negative side of the ledger is that what is meant by culture is often far less obvious.

Two things about culture can be stated with certainty. The first: culture changes, whether those at the helm want it to or not. The second: the notion that culture is about everyone acting in the same way is fraught with problems (an inability to accept ideas from the outside being but one). Whereas it's true that culture defines the range of behaviors that are acceptable, it is not about creating an environment where everyone, Borg-like,[1] adheres to a narrow set of rules or protocols. Indeed, a pattern of rigid behavior reinforced by punishment of those who challenge the rules is the first building block in the formation of a cult. Add a philosophy of exclusion and a charismatic leader who has a unique answer to the ills of society, and *all* of the pieces are in place. By comparison, culture is a container for diversity…not unlimited and unbridled diversity (chaos), but a context where acceptable and agreed differences are encouraged, even nurtured.

Shaping the culture[2] demands an understanding of two critical forces: (1) those elements that anchor the organization where it is (anchors); and (2) those forces that move it forward (drivers). By and large, organizations spend a lot of time with the latter and do their best to ignore the former.

Foremost among the "anchors" are the history of the enterprise, mindsets, symbolism, ritual, myth, story, the organization's heroes, established language, how power is distributed (as in structure), and the values being acted out by those in leadership positions. As always, what a leader *does* is *far* more important than anything he/she might *say*.

The "drivers" describe *tomorrow's success*: the vision, what will be rewarded, and the emerging

---

[1] Well known to Star Trek fans, the Borg are a formidable foe of the Federation. The Borgs' actions are controlled by their collective consciousness. To "be at one with Borg" is to give up one's free will.

[2] A far more realistic term than "changing the culture."

leadership competencies. Any one of these issues should ideally be labeled, "If taken inappropriately could be dangerous for your organization's health." Leadership competencies are a case in point: generic competencies are a great way to define leadership success but, unless complemented by characteristics of success that are role-specific, are akin to a blanket that has warp but little or no weft[3]…it might suggest warmth but at the first breath of wind its utility vanishes. (For more on this topic see Chapter Six.)

Those who work in the enterprise pick up the movement of, or clash between, the cultural anchors and the drivers as cultural "noise." This stream of sound constantly bombards employees at every level. For those who know how to listen, it is a constant buzz that engulfs and fills the white space on the organization chart. The real action has nothing to do with what's in the boxes! Organizational savvy is the capacity to interpret this noise. Shaping the culture is to change its pitch, content and volume. Some sound makes the greatest difference when it is merely a whisper. At other times the space that surrounds people serves the organization best when the timbre and resonance being emitted fills the background so that it reaches an emotional crescendo. Leadership is to know the difference and to act accordingly.

A sub-set of the noise being transmitted is the "message" that supports, or works against, collaboration. Leaders cannot make collaboration happen by telling people to collaborate. This is like putting an advertisement in the paper and demanding that the person who stole your wallet return it because you need the money that was inside. Collaboration is about *mutual* self-interest. Collaboration happens when the context supports it. Collaboration takes off when it creates value for all those involved. Collaboration becomes reality only if and when **the organizational noise endorses it**.

For collaboration to become a reality, for the organizational noise to support collaboration, a number of things have to be in place:

- The organization's vision has to embrace collaboration.
- Collaboration must be measured.
- The organization's leadership competencies have to define collaboration as being central to leadership success.
- Leaders have to become skilled in storytelling and use the stories to celebrate the success of collaborative initiatives. (See Chapter Four, "Leaders are storytellers.")
- The organization's values have to reinforce collaboration, which means that those in key leadership roles who do not display a collaborative mindset are confronted and, if need be, separated from the organization.
- The organization structure has to enable rather than frustrate collaboration.

[3] The thread crossing and woven into the warp to make the web.

- The symbolism (imagery, language, design) used in branding, communication, leadership development, and web-based learning must capture the spirit of collaboration.
- The traditional language of "team" has to give way to the language of "connectivity."

Those in positions of power can talk about collaboration all they want. They can pull their hair out and stamp their feet. They can issue edicts by the score. The pragmatic reality is that no matter what leaders say, if the music that plays in the background does not support collaboration, few will take the time, effort, or risk to actually go out of their way to create value by working together. Only a fool, or a pedestrian who has imbibed too much of Scotland's most famous product, walks when the light is red!

2. Do the assumptions that underline the leadership process support collaboration?

Until the late fifteenth century, the inhabitants of the Yucatan Peninsula represented a vibrant culture of more than a dozen major cities. The center of their world was Tikal, a metropolis of over 100,000 people covering an area of 23 miles. Today the Maya are an impoverished people, stripped of dignity and degraded by four centuries of exploitation, denial and repression.

Part of the explanation for their pauper status is that they used Stone-Age technology: little bronze, no iron and no practical use of the wheel. Slash-and-burn farming also led to irreparable land erosion.

There is, however, another significant piece of the puzzle. The Mayan measurement of time was kept on a cycle called *katums* (13 x 20-year periods). They perceived time not as a process of linear progression, but as a series of interlocking cycles forming repeating patterns. Because of this the Maya assumed that the Spanish could not be vanquished until a full cycle of 360 years had elapsed…exactly, as it turned out, the length of time the Spanish did stay in power. The Mayan calendar was so rooted in their culture that the ensuing fatalism and high level of resignation meant a complete abdication of action. The Mayan nation floundered, not so much because of elements found wanting in their civilization but because of the very assumptions that underpinned their culture.

Collaboration becomes reality only if and when the organizational noise endorses it.

Moving ahead 500 years… are things so different? How many people voted approvingly with their wallets because a 24-year-old technology evangelist said that the dot-com world was the cutting edge of a NEW economy? Who would have believed that a nation touted as the model of democracy would have to wait several weeks to anoint its president because its voting machines were a product of its own technological Stone Age? How we think is how we act. What we believe drives what we determine is possible. Collaboration inevitably flounders when the organization is wired in ways that work against connectivity.

The following, in particular, handcuff an organization's capacity to act collectively:

- *The assumption that providing the tools for warehousing and transmitting knowledge means that people will actually share that knowledge.* Assuming that knowledge is a commodity leads to the false premise that transferring knowledge is a simple transaction. As a result, processes aimed at sharing best practice – groupware, study tours, innovation conferences, knowledge webs – often turn out to be a poor investment. Accessibility gets confused with awareness, and content viewed as a meaningful substitute for commitment. What gets overlooked is the human factor. We attach a high level of emotional value (pride, ownership, even a sense of identity) to that which resides in our head or rests in our fingertips. The outcome: collaboration is far more than a mechanistic process that can be orchestrated by introducing the right "tools." It is a very personal experience requiring trust and, not infrequently, face-to-face interaction. In the midst of war, Churchill and Roosevelt still found it necessary to meet.

- *The premise that consensus and collaboration are terms that are essentially interchangeable.* Consensus is to "connect" those who are party to a decision as a means to build collective buy-in. To wit: the individual is expected to suppress his/her thinking to the better good of "the team." Consensus works wonderfully well if the challenge is to improve on that which is already in place. Consensus is a less seductive process, however, when breakthrough thinking is demanded. Consensus is the art of acquiescence. Collaboration is a place where mavericks are nurtured and wild ideas are listened to with reverence. Consensus exploits what is there. Collaboration starts by asking, "What is missing?" The more successful the past, the more demanding the question! Consensus aims to fill the glass. Collaboration starts by emptying it, and if that doesn't create a new view of the world... smashing it. If consensus is the smooth and graceful movements of the waltz, collaboration is the echoing staccato of the tap-dance. Consensus is the rich and deep tone of a French horn. Collaboration is the sound of fingernails being scraped on a blackboard. Consensus is the blending of muted pastels in a Victorian watercolor. Collaboration is the jagged and violent juxtaposition of color and texture found in a Jackson Pollock original. Consensus seeks to smooth out the emotional tension...collaboration embraces it as fundamental to the nature of reinvention. Consensus says, "Let's work with what we've got." Collaboration is a faithful partner to its alter ego, creativity.

  > *Consensus is the rich and deep tone of a French horn. Collaboration is the sound of fingernails being scraped on a blackboard.*

- *A mindset that assumes competition and collaboration cannot coexist.* The traditional notion of competition is to protect, to put up barriers, and to communicate exclusively on a need-to-know basis. Not everyone supports this presumption. Prime movers and legendary competitors are invariably the ones who throw their doors open the widest!

Toyota freely shares its world-beating, smart manufacturing systems with competitors. Disney, Nokia, Wal-Mart, Virgin, General Electric and Dell similarly tell the world what they do and more importantly…how they do it.

Fierce competitors seek collaboration because reaching out and seeking new ideas is, of necessity, a way of life. They understand that the spirit of collaboration lies in a natural curiosity that can never be a one-way process. Leaders who live in a cocoon of assumed security act on the misplaced belief that they are self-contained masters of their own destiny. Those who sit at the court of the Red Queen see collaboration – even with competitors – as central to their survival.

3. Does the structure work for or against collaboration?

A malaise facing today's businesses, big and small, is that the stresses placed on the organization's structural architecture far outstrip what we currently know about organization design. Effective structure should meet the **FLAT** test:

(1) Ensure **F**ocus…marshal the organization's resources in pursuit of the vision.

(2) Describe as few decision-making **L**evels as possible…every unnecessary organizational level halves the effectiveness of communication.

(3) Facilitate **A**gility…new pathways and networks are created in response to unique customer needs and new opportunity. Because some decisions (e.g. selling off parts of the business) can and should only be made by those who have a helicopter view of the total organization, the suggestion that organizations can strip out hierarchy entirely is a laudable, but entirely impractical ideal.

(4) Make **T**ime a competitive advantage…the organization can deliver its value proposition consistently faster than the competition.

Taking into account that the modern organization has been around since the turn of the last century, the number of organization forms that a leader can draw on is remarkably small. Although differing in style and cut, six basic organizational models pretty well exhaust the options. (*See Figure two.*)

It should not be assumed that an organization should have one unifying, common organization model. (See Chapter Four.) Leadership is, in no small measure, the ability to effectively embrace different ways to organize. It goes without saying that some organizational design options support collaboration more than others.

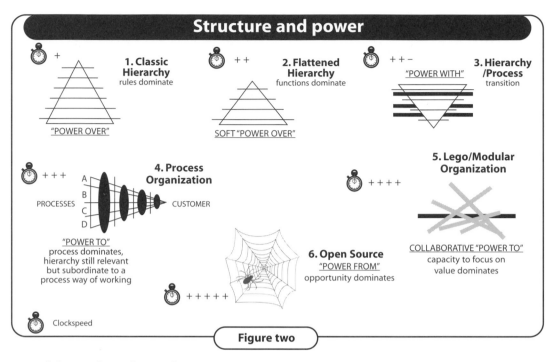

Figure two

Model one: classic hierarchy

In the Age of Steel the organization, as with everything else, was built to last. Multiple levels, rigid, durable and inflexible, the classic hierarchy was designed to carry heavy traffic to a predictable and largely unchanging destination.

The mechanistic turn of mind that lay behind early industrialization led to several "obvious" conclusions:

- Efficiency was an outcome of breaking the work down into its smallest constituent parts.

- Controlling those needed to do the work meant that employees – with little training – had to be interchangeable.

- Complex and unwieldy processes were needed to knit the otherwise disconnected elements of work together.

- The rigidity, to say nothing of the complexity, could only be overcome if coordinators, multiple levels of supervisors and an army of administrators were employed.

- Strategy belonged at the center.

Top leaders looked down on their domain confident that efficiency, consistency and good order were the outcome of breaking work down into a series of micro tasks and responsibilities. The old dog learned a couple of new tricks when the divisional structure was created in the 1930s and international businesses were added in the 1950s.

In truth, the classic hierarchy worked because in the world of the blind the one-eyed man is king. It was the best system around. There is another reason: the informal organization that ebbed and flowed within its rigid structures (unless self-interest suggested otherwise) found creative ways to bend and/or circumvent the rules. Employees discovered how to beat the bureaucracy by painting outside the established lines of authority. Indeed, if for one day the organization had even attempted to operate along the lines dictated by the formal organization chart, the gears would have ground to a screeching halt.

The reality is that **every** organization is a series of networks.[4] The dilemma: the natural propensity for human beings to form collaborative networks is frustrated by the rigidity that accompanies formal hierarchy. Stalin failed to understand this when he modeled the Soviet economy on the highly-centralized and fully-integrated manufacturing system developed by Henry Ford. The more efficient centralized planning became, the less effective it was destined to be. The irony: the worm that ate away and eventually overwhelmed totalitarianism (aided by Star Wars, Coca-Cola and MuchMusic) was the one thing that the old guard in the Soviet Union coveted most in capitalism.

Model two: flattened hierarchy

The multi-tiered hierarchical model started to fall apart when the nations defeated in World War II (Japan and Germany) let loose the product of their own industrial miracle on an unsuspecting Detroit and Coventry. The result: starting in the 1980s, massive cost reduction in the form of restructuring and downsizing. It was the birth of a leaner – some would say meaner – hierarchy. "Slash-and-burn" was in.

An already stripped-down hierarchy came under further attack when organizations started to get the message on quality ("If Japan can, why can't we?"). Talking to the customer was something of a revelation all on its own… "Hey, can you believe it? They are telling us we have to do better or they will go elsewhere!" It was the end of an era when to lead was to believe "If we make it *they* will come." Managing from the "inside-out" had enjoyed its last hurrah. It was also our introduction to an immutable law of economics: Third World work (in the form of simplistic jobs) will always flow to the Third World.

---

[4] Mary Parker Follett was writing about networked organizations in the 1920s.

Model three: hierarchy/process

The "quality revolution" improved quality but did little to address systemic inefficiencies in the system, e.g. reduce cycle times. We had stretched the classic organization but we were still trying to get the elephant to dance. It wasn't until quality bumped into process that new thinking evolved. Hello, process reengineering!

Flawed, insomuch as it was often based on the self-defeating tactic of asking employees to shape a stick with which they would then be beaten to death, process reengineering contained within it the seeds of a structural revolution. Except… it was much easier to reengineer the old silos than to reorganize around the key processes. Except…few had the will to take on the power of the functional hierarchy. Except… it was assumed that changing the structure would, by itself, change the prevailing functional mindset.

Clearly there is a transition needed in moving from hierarchy to process. There is value in evolving from function to process. And a degree of hierarchy is essential. The dilemma: you cannot give *equal weight* to process thinking and functional hierarchy beyond the transition phase. Attempts to run function and process in tandem as co-dependent structures (hard matrix) can have only one outcome: organizational gridlock.

Model four: the process organization

In the world of process, hierarchy lives but moves into the background, silos are demolished, and the value chains rule (soft matrix).

It should not be assumed that the process organization is a mature option. An effective process way of working can be handicapped by any of the following factors:

- Lack of discipline in defining the core competencies.[5]
- A reluctance to fold into the core processes work that traditionally resides within a functional hierarchy.
- The challenge of transforming the traditional supervisory (meister) role into that of team leader.
- An incentive system that does not reward collaboration.
- Those who work within the process still not being given an opportunity to do whole jobs… a mechanistic mind-set wedded to a process way to work.
- The language of elitism e.g. "the process champion." Process leader is a far more apt description.

---

[5] In doing so, step one is to define the emerging value proposition.

- Failure to create a common, process-focused database.

- Lack of effective communication between those in the different core processes; as a result, hierarchical silos are replaced by horizontal bunkers.

The process organization creates the opportunity for innovation and entrepreneurship to flourish. For this to become a reality, those who drive the processes have to be given far more scope and authority than has been traditionally comfortable for many leaders. Ideas have to be allowed to bubble up from the bottom, strategy has to be devolved to those who interface with the customer, and "freedom to act" has to become more than a statement in the company's annual report. Perhaps most important of all, leaders have to become comfortable with ambiguity, and understand that before anything can change, a whole lot of "letting go" has to happen – mostly by them.

Model five: the Lego[6]/modular organization

In the vast majority of organizations there are four core business processes:
  (1) *The offering process*, which aligns ideas, design, sales, and marketing with the customer's emerging needs;

  (2) *The build process*, which creates the products and services needed to serve the customer;

  (3) *The distribution process*, which gets the product and/or service to the customer on time; and

  (4) *The management process*, which is the human and systems capital needed to create, support and fix breakdowns in the infrastructure.

Savvy leaders ask at which one of these do we excel, and why should we not outsource *absolutely everything else*. If someone else can do it better, why not give them the work? One multinational giant has decided that a global consulting group can do a better role of managing the development and retention of its human capital. No industry is immune. In the pharmaceutical industry the question becomes, can we really excel at drug discovery, clinical trials and everything in between? The prognosis: an unprecedented level of out-sourcing (and with it, collaboration) lies ahead.

There are several caveats that come with a modular (Lego) mentality:

- Can those being asked to do the outsourced work do it better than the host?

- Are the spirit, the tools and the organization in place to facilitate effective collaboration?

- Will it cost more? Legions of CIOs were persuaded to outsource the company's

[6]LEGO is the trademark of the Denmark-based LEGO Company. The LEGO Company was built upon a vision that we should nurture the child within every one of us.

information technology, only to find that the lack of focus, the time spent addressing problems, and reduced service added up to far more than the savings involved.

- What will be the impact on the core competencies we retain? What differentiates the organization is rarely limited to one process. It is far more likely to be a bundle of skills and attributes drawn from different processes.

Model six: open source

The inspiration for this final model comes from the revolution in organizational thinking Linus Torvalds created when he unleashed Linux. He was an unknown student at the University of Helsinki when, in 1991, he started distributing his homemade operating system for free. By inviting other programmers to work with his source code and share changes and fixes – which they did by the thousand – he and his on-line peers drove a stake into the soft underbelly of companies like Microsoft and Sun. Torvalds created the first in what has emerged as an avalanche of loosely connected, on-line communities all working towards a common cause, linked not by wealth creation but by the pure joy of creating.

The strength of the open source organization is the blazing speed at which it can create and redefine itself, combined with the lack of formal infrastructure needed to sustain it.

What distinguishes the open source model is that it can be spun and re-spun into different shapes and with different content. Unfettered by past practice, its lifeblood is opportunity and innovation. And like the spider's silky ambush, a single vibration, no matter how slight, is immediately communicated to every knot and pathway on the web. The strength of the open source organization is the blazing speed at which it can create and redefine itself, combined with the lack of formal infrastructure needed to sustain it. Of course real-time, constantly changing, many-to-many networks, when added to a multiple-roles way to organize are final proof, for many, that the lunatics have finally taken over the asylum.

*   *   *   *   *

The characteristics of the **FLAT** organizations have already been suggested. Other design considerations include the organization's value proposition, the need to stimulate innovation, the well of human capital available, the value of collaboration between the separate businesses, and the speed at which the market(s) change in which the organization operates. In a Red Queen World, speed becomes the overriding imperative. When any single business reinvents its clockspeed,[7] the clockspeed changes instantly, and irrevocably, for everyone else in that industry.

---

[7] A term coined by Charles Fine in his book *Clockspeed* (1998).

All relationships are about power. It matters not whether we are describing interactions that are one-on-one, or the complex informal dynamic of a large enterprise. Structure is just another way to say, "This is the way power is distributed around here."

- The classic hierarchy *(see Figure two)* assumes that employees cannot, and should not, be trusted. **"Power over"**[8] is a natural extension of a culture devoid of basic trust.

- In the flattened hierarchy the need for greater initiative – even though the work is still broken down into micro tasks – means that a kinder, gentler approach prevails. An emphasis on "human resources" leads to what can be described as **"soft power over."**

- In the transitional stage between hierarchy and process, a degree of power sharing becomes necessary. Top leaders still hold the reins of power but without creating space for team initiative, the process element of the structure cannot take off (**"power with"**).[9]

- The process organization can only work if power is passed to those within the processes (**"power to"**).[10] In the Lego organization "power to" takes on a collaborative face.

- Open source organizations are perfectly described as **"power from."**[11] Indeed, by definition power flows from anywhere to anywhere.

At each organization shift the leadership style must change accordingly. Changing the structure without making the necessary adjustment in the way power is accessed guarantees that even small change initiatives will flounder. Leadership is thus about understanding power. Here the plot thickens. A large organization has several (possibly all) of the structures described, within its boundaries. Leadership in a Red Queen World is to successfully straddle all of these organizational forms. (See Chapter Four.)

The classic organization is hardwired and durable but has a turning circle reminiscent of a battleship. The process organization creates whole jobs, knits teams together, drives down cost, reduces cycle times, and instills workers with a common understanding of how the business creates value for the customer. It moves fast, but its tracks (processes), once laid down, are not easily, or swiftly, ripped up and then "engineered" to follow a different path. The open source organization moves at the speed of light and turns on a dime. It is a level of agility, however, that comes at a cost. Freedom to act equals significant and ongoing investment in human capital. The greater the freedom to act, the greater the investment.

Changing the structure without making the necessary adjustment in the way power is accessed guarantees that even small change initiatives will flounder.

In a perverse way, the open source organization returns full cycle to the informal organization that allowed the organization

[8] In Chapter Four "power over" and "soft power over" are represented by a T1 organization.
[9] In Chapter Four "power with" is represented by an organization that straddles T1 and T2.
[10] In Chapter Four "power to" is represented by a T2 organization.
[11] In Chapter Four "power from" is represented by a T3 organization.

pyramid (classic hierarchy) to work. If this proves anything, it is that the best organization design is nothing more than finding a way for people to work together that replicates how they would actually choose to work together. Put more succinctly: leadership is mostly about stripping out that which gets in people's way. It also provides undeniable evidence that organizations aren't about bricks and mortar, machines, or even technology. An organization, when all the rhetoric is forgotten, is simply the sum of its people.

4. Is there easy access to the organization's "village green" ?

The scene: a small village pub in the English midlands. At the bar, a local doctor is talking to a farm worker about European farm subsidies. By the door, tourists are engaged in a good-natured argument with one of the locals about the merits (or lack therein) of English cooking. Gardening is the subject of conversation in the next room. Of course, those pillars of conversation, the weather, sex and politics are never far from the surface. Unlike London's so-called "Gentleman's Clubs," nothing is off-limits.

What makes this eclectic group of people want to spend time together? It's certainly not financial gain. In most instances it's not the quality of the beer. There is no entertainment except that which is self-organized…skittles, darts, and dominoes. And a jukebox would empty the place faster than fire. Yet night after night this is where the village meets. This is where ideas are floated, where confidences are shared, and where advice is freely given.

If there is a currency of acceptance it lies in common courtesy, a willingness to listen, and the capacity to be oneself. Status, power, wealth all appear to be secondary to character and openness. Moreover, it is common space. All – save those who are underage – are welcome.

Part of what brings people to the pub is mutual self-interest. Those who spend the evening there both give and receive. There is also something deep within the human psyche that seeks community; that yearns for a sense of belonging; that draws meaning out of being part of something larger than oneself. Somewhere in the mix is identity. Without the pub, the assemblage of houses that lies within walking distance would hardly qualify for the term "village."

There is much here for the modern organization. Collaboration and community go hand in hand. Both, however, are nurtured and brought to full flowering by the quality of the space available. None of this is new; organizations that have enacted collaboration know this only too well. As for the rest – they would be well advised to copy shamelessly that which others have discovered. What follows are examples of the "village green." That the list is incomplete goes without saying. As you read the examples you might like to think about the village green, or lack of it, in your own organization.

- *Make the mission bigger than individual eg*os…The human genome project created a process where researchers published their research on the Internet for others to build on.

- *Know where the breakthroughs ar*e…Ford posts five to eight weekly new best practices from all its assembly plants. The information includes not only the source of the best practice but video and other support material that allow ease of understanding.

- *Pool the organization's knowledge*…Ernst and Young has created a series of databases under the title of the *Knowledge Web* to capture the outcome and learning derived from consulting projects around the world. These consulting activities are organized into like arenas (merger, compensation, expatriate taxation, and performance management) and the very best work is bundled into succinct packages that are easy to download. These so-called "power packs" not only distil what would otherwise be an overwhelming body of data into buckets of excellence, but highlight how to contact internal experts in the field, throw up the best articles written on the topic, and outline past mistakes. British Petroleum relies on a similar knowledge repository.

- *Make breakthrough-thinking fun*…Sodexho, the French-based services giant (whose Sodexho Marriott Division alone employs over 100,000 people and supervises another 50,000 in the delivery of corporate, school and hospital meal/cafeteria services) organizes a highly successful annual innovation competition. Local, regional, and international events draw out the winners who enjoy not only great prestige, but also the opportunity to travel to other parts of the organization to share their ideas.

- *Capture and share the stories*…Southwest Airlines has created a standing team of cultural ambassadors…over 100 trained storytellers whose role, in addition to their regular duties, is to perpetuate the organization's spirit.

- *Look in new places* …The US Marines, in determining how to respond to its new role in the world, have conducted a series of in-depth study tours. What makes their approach interesting is that among the groups they have been studying are foreign exchange dealers on Wall Street, Wal-Mart, Southwest Airlines, and 3M.

- *Break the mold*…In the mid-1990s Bill Gross, the founder of Idealab, turned the venture capital concept on its head. Instead of raising money and waiting for businesses to come to him he decided that a better approach was to have his team generate the ideas, build the business model, go out and recruit the talent and then raise equity for each company.

- *Rethink who is on the team*…Few can match the competitive spirit of Richard Noble, the self-styled British eccentric, who broke the world land speed record in 1983 (633 m.p.h.). For his second attempt at the record Richard chose not to drive but to manage the overall attempt. He was rewarded in 1997 when his driver, RAF Squadron Leader

Andy Green, crashed through the sound barrier at 763 m.p.h. And what was unique about Richard's leadership? His funding came in large measure from thousands of enthusiastic subscribers on the Internet. At one point, when the effort to break the record was stalled because of a major fuel bill, the team's appeal for funds yielded 15,000 pounds Sterling in a single day and 400,000 pounds Sterling in less than twenty days. When corporate sponsors walked away Richard didn't give up, he dug his heels in and decided he wasn't prepared to live with other people's definition of "team."

*   *   *   *   *

Spartan valor at Thermopylae was the outcome of intense discipline, physical endurance and sustained training. It was, for example, a serious breach of the Spartan code for a warrior to lose his sword. The punishment that followed was swift and harsh. Lose a shield, however, and the punishment was worse – death. A sword was for the warrior's own protection. The shield, on the other hand, also protected the soldiers on either side. In the cult of spiritual courage that was Sparta, collaborate or die was no idle threat! Thus, let no one suggest that collaboration is new, a fad, or worse, one more here today – gone tomorrow dimension of the leadership experience.

The challenge for the leader isn't to merely promote the need but to deliver the pragmatism involved in making collaboration happen. Clearly there is no one solution. It would be foolish if those seeking to build a creative and collaborative business environment chose to ignore the power of culture; overlook the need to shape the belief system of the organization; turn a blind eye to the reality that there is a new definition of what is meant by the term "team"; fail to recognize the influence of the organization's structure; and/or lack the will to both re-seed the village green and repave the roads that lead to it.

What to do differently on Monday

1. To what extent does the culture in your organization support collaboration? Where needed revisit: the vision, how collaboration is measured, the organization's values, the leadership competencies and the metaphors used to support collaboration.

2. Is collaboration part of how the organization acts? Is the human aspect of collaboration fully factored into the introduction of new networking technology? Look to your own area of influence, act on those things that can be done to (re)instill the human face of collaboration.

3. Is the difference between consensus and collaboration fully understood? Make sure your own team understands the difference and acts accordingly.

4. Does the structure support collaboration? In the race for tomorrow, discussion regarding structure has been pushed to one side.   Make structure a strategic issue.   Make the way the business organizes and moves knowledge around and across the organization central to how the business competes. Make structure central to the leadership conversation.

5. Is there easy access to the "village green"? No village green, no collaboration. Work with others to create new village greens.   Strive to make the ones that already exist operate effectively.

Chapter three

Organizations that don't learn, don't earn

Book One
Leadership of the Organization

> *"Come to the edge, He said.*
> *They said, We are afraid.*
> *Come to the edge, He said.*
> *They came.*
> *He pushed them...and they flew."*
>
> Guillaume Apollinaire

Going to the edge

The heat rose from the black tarmac in heavy, relentless waves. Even though the sun was still sometime away from its mid-day climax, the thermometer was well into the high nineties (36C+). Evidence of the debilitating effect of the heat lay with the boxes of bottled water – now almost empty – neatly stacked ready for departure. No doubt relishing a brief respite in the chilled confines of the hotel, the driver signaled he would return for more. An encouraging cheer accompanied his swift exit.

Anyone who has been in Orlando in the middle of summer knows that the pool and/or an air-conditioned room are where the smart crowd while away the days. And yet an unannounced observer would have seen a group of thirty "visitors" from eight countries fully attired in firefighting equipment. The fashion statement of the day: the latest Kevlar[1] heavy-duty pants and jacket, fire-resistant hood, helmet, mask,

---

[1] Kevlar is a flame-resistant industrial textile that weighs very little but is five times stronger than steel.

boots and gloves.   And, of course, to set the ensemble off – full breathing apparatus.

To those of a rational temperament, the mere thought of standing around in the attire described summons up images of heat exhaustion. The team didn't have time to be exhausted. They were being put through the first ten weeks of firefighter training – in a single day. Their instructors: seasoned fire chiefs. The venue: one of the most advanced firefighting academies in North America.

The morning training started in the classroom at first light but quickly moved into the yard. The initial work was in pairs on the fire hoses. Dragging a water-filled hose and keeping the heavy stream of white water pointed at the target is tough, physical labor. With gallons of pressurized water pushing the hose backwards, it is as if an unseen hand is at work. That said, water is still a firefighter's best buddy. But forget the movies. The team quickly discovered that you fight a fire on your belly. Two of the women in the class were thrown around by the watery blast as if they were riding an out of control power cable. Determined and committed, they stuck to their task. Through sheer willpower they brought the "current" under their spell. Looking on with a confidence born out of military training, several of the men exuded an aura of "Let's get the job done." When their time came, however, they were only too pleased to accept advice from "the ladies."

The final challenge of the morning was to bellycrawl across 150 feet of grass guided only by sound. With the mask blackened out and the white noise of the oxygen flow dulling the senses, this was no easy task. The chief provided that extra edge when he remarked that accidentally turning the oxygen onto full flow would likely "blow your teeth down your throat." The team was at the edge; or so they thought!

Mid-day brought a stay from the heat but not from the challenge. The group spent the afternoon discussing what it meant to be a leader. Several key points emerged. In a Red Queen World sustainable competitive advantage is a myth. Constructive destruction must become a way of life. Someone out there is about to reinvent the game. Strategy is about retaliating first and has little to do with "the plan." The question was posed: Why do people follow a leader? Discussion moved from concept to practice. Examples surfaced.   Issues such as vision, living the values, learning, trust, authenticity and openness were tabled. The underlying agenda: "What specifically can I do differently on Monday?"

The morning session was deliberately not discussed. That it was about the head and the hand would become apparent when issues of the heart and spirit moved to the fore in the evening. The team was about to go to the edge. They were about to go into the dragon's throat.

Man is programmed from his earliest origins to fear fire. We are hardwired to run from its terrifying touch. The Burn Room knew of no such contract. A square concrete bunker laden with technology, the Burn Room can be programmed to simulate anything a firefighter comes across in the field. On this evening an apartment fire was on the menu.

The reason for staying close to the ground became immediately apparent. The steel-plated ceiling of the Burn Room reaches temperatures of 1200 degrees Fahrenheit. The thermal layering of the clothing bursts into flames at much lower temperatures than this. At head height, where the temperature reaches 400-500 degrees Fahrenheit, it can melt the helmet's face shield. Only at ground level where the temperature is a "cool" 200 degrees is there any degree of comfort. Even this comfort was denied when one of the additional evening instructors gave the advice, "Attack the fire and it will reward you, hold back and you will be punished." Heart and spirit were suddenly part of the mix.

The team members readied themselves. They were about to go into the Burn Room in teams of two. An instructor was to accompany each team. Teamwork moved to the fore. Everyone checked each other's dress. Bare skin would mean a serious burn. The dragon beckoned.

Nothing can prepare you for entering the Burn Room and hearing the hard metallic clang of the steel door behind you. You feel trapped. Suddenly your partner becomes your lifeline and your instructor a guardian angel. Amid the smoke and overpowering heat the morning training represents the difference between action and panic. The mask mists up – why did no one mention this? From the safety of the area close to the door, you set the hose on the flames. The hose displays behavior reminiscent of a giant python that missed its lunch. Rather than die down, the flames increase in intensity. It is your turn to take the lead on the hose. Your instructor tells you to stand up and attack the fire. From somewhere – even weeks later you have no idea where – a surge of adrenaline makes you plunge forward. You are pumping water onto the flames. The heat is intense. It is more than intense…it is overwhelming. Welcome to man's worst nightmare. The flames eventually die down. But heat from the steam only drives the temperature higher. You remember the chief saying that steam delivers the worst burns of all. Your ears are burning. The instructor taps you on the shoulder. You back out – thankfully. Your appreciation of those who do this for a living increases a thousand-fold. You take your mask off with gloved hand, amazed that the suit and the helmet are too hot to touch. Fresh air never tasted so good. **Welcome to the edge!**

The teams enter the Burn Room twice, the second time without smoke but with conditions that simulate a fire rolling across the ceiling and moving behind the firefighters (backdraft). A final "fight" is enacted in the night air. The challenge: a 60-foot oil fire. In the dark it is spectacular. The problem: the dragon doesn't play by the rules. When she should have died she attacks from the side. When she seems mute she drives in from the rear. The Queen is here! The day ends at 11.30pm. Sleep is no problem.

Learning as play

Let us step back and consider what the firefighting is really all about. The leadership development being described is a far cry from the classroom presentation, case study, or even the well-crafted simulation. It is learning that deliberately plays in the heart and spirit space. Challenging, emotionally impactful, physically tiring, it is learning that will live in the hearts and minds of those who went through it for the rest of their lives. Even months later leaders talk of these sessions as if they had occurred yesterday.

The current explosion of interest in learning that uses outdoor events notwithstanding, designing experiential learning activities is an "art form" not easily mastered. There is, for example, a wide gulf between *play as learning* and *learning as play*. The former assumes that events such as Outward Bound, ropes programs, blind-walk, go-kart racing (the list is virtually endless), provide a common platform from which a wide range of learning can be squeezed. Play as learning builds from the event. Learning as play focuses on the outcome. One is painting by the numbers. The other starts from blank canvas.

In play as learning, typical facilitation questions are: "What did you learn about yourself by jumping from that pole?" "In what way did being blindfolded teach you something about leadership?" In fact these are not such simple questions. The participant has the complex task to first draw personal meaning from the learning experience, then make the leap from the event to the real world then, finally, compare the two – all in real-time. The resulting conclusions are likely to be shallow observations, more about not looking bad in front of his/her peers than defining any personal change agenda. The concern is compounded when the imagery created by the event is misaligned with the journey the participants are on. Go-karts do little to foster collaboration. A ropes program is a poor representation of speed. And from a leadership perspective, "blind" followship is behavior that few would seek to deliberately foster.

Play as learning starts with the event and largely ignores the organization's journey. It is one size fits all. Learning as play starts from an entirely different proposition. The event is secondary. Participant learning shapes the event. There are several important ramifications that flow from learning as play:

1. The nature, speed, and scope of the organization's change journey must be fully understood.

2. The journey needs to be captured by a metaphor that fits the context (e.g. the Red Queen; the head, the hand, the heart, and the spirit).

3. The event must be specifically designed to make the metaphor live.

4. The imagery used, the environment chosen, the language, the rhythm, and pace of the event all have to fold into the metaphor.

5. Where the organization has a well-defined brand, the learning metaphor and the brand have to be a natural fit.

6. The facilitators must display behavior consistent with the outcomes the learning event is designed to create. We will return to this point.

In "making the metaphor live," the learning moves significantly beyond skills and knowledge. Metaphor-anchored learning reframes mindsets and delivers a common sense of identity. The "art" comes not in merely replicating what others have done elsewhere but in creating a unique experience. In our own work this has led to a wide range of learning interventions. To name a few: firefighting, tap dancing, bull fighting, bush walks in Australia, a game park in South Africa, antique ocean-going yachts, rifle shooting, ice-hockey training camp, rescue missions, building a log cabin, various forms of motor sports from trucks to Formula Four, bell-ringing, martial arts, cooking, bow-shooting, singing events, wine-tasting in Château Village, Native American sweat lodges, and a wide range of survival and competitive experiences. To make the shark and dolphin metaphor come alive we have visited Sea-World several times, and literally have had dinner with the sharks and dessert with the dolphins.

Tap dancing is a good example of the value of learning as play. Designed specifically to support work with a team of Swiss Germans, the somewhat formal and rigid persona of the group was totally transformed by four hours of tap. The theatre of learning became the body, not the head. Thinking gave way to feeling. The head had become used to intellectualizing and challenging ideas. The body was emotional space waiting to be filled. And change is, after all, an emotional experience. Moreover, learning anchored in the nervous system becomes hardwired. With the Swiss group the tap dancing was followed by a session that involved each member of the top team giving each other member candid, face-to-face feedback. Before the dance experience this could never have taken place. As it turned out this became a pivotal experience in their change work. At the time of writing, the business is the number one performer in their industry.

Another example is how the top team of a global organization based in Finland explored the difference between service and serving. Impressed with the way the guest tents for the World Hockey Championship in Finland had been catered, they met with the caterers. What they heard was that the success of the catering team's contribution was based on two critical issues. The first, attention paid to recruiting employees for the project. The second, a quality described as "hinku." In Finnish, hinku isn't just the act of serving, it's a passion to serve. It's a way to serve with dignity that enriches the server. Service is what people expect. It is what has been agreed. Serving encompasses not just what has been agreed, but how people *feel* about the experience.

To make the difference live, the top team was invited – from around the world – to an early breakfast at one of the company's most remote locations. However, upon arriving, instead of being fed they were handed aprons. They were about to serve breakfast to frontline employees. The breakfast turned out to be a humorous and good-natured disaster with one grinning worker complaining to the President about a thumbprint in his eggs. Early on in the discussions with the catering firm we became aware that the young executive in charge of the hockey event was also a champion ballroom dancer, and thus it was at 7.00am on a very dark, very cold morning, with a foot of snow outside, and to the accompaniment of a Strauss waltz, employees were invited to dance.

Following the breakfast fiasco the team was trained by the catering company in how to *really* serve. Small group discussion focusing around a series of prepared breakthrough questions followed. The CEO of the catering firm shared best practice. The implications for the organization were significant. At lunch the team was again put in charge of the meal. Perfection! Or at least close to it. The Finnish business involved grew its service business tenfold.

One event that was especially impactful took place in Brisbane, Australia. At 8.00am the leadership team was handed $300, and told they were to double it, by legal means, by the end of the day. That evening they returned with over $1,500. They did so by approaching the local children's hospital and becoming a legal charity for a day. The $300 "seed money" went into collection boxes. Perhaps even more impressive, this was only one of five or six ideas that would have worked. The intended learning around innovation, thinking outside of the box, and acting fast was apparent in everything the team attempted. When a representative from the hospital came to collect the money that same day she came with a "thank you" signed by a little boy dying of leukemia. There was not a dry eye in the house. There was no need to explain that leadership was about heart and spirit. There was no need to talk in abstract terms about "community." The certificate from the hospital still hangs proudly in the entrance of their corporate office.

In framing the learning in a meaningful metaphor, new behavior is reinforced – at both a conscious and sub-conscious level. The metaphor becomes both the container for shared learning and a platform from which new questions evolve. Forget the mental gymnastics of stop, analyze, compare, and conclude. There is no need for participants to fake it in the hope that eventually they will make it. The participants are living the change demanded!

Facilitation

Learning often benefits greatly by bringing on board an outstanding facilitator. The dictionary describes facilitation as, "to make easier." Would that were always the case! Facilitation is like good acting: the better the facilitator, the easier it seems. There are a lot of bad actors. In like manner, the choice of facilitator needs very careful thought.

Figure three outlines four distinct styles of facilitation. The path of least resistance, the style that evokes the least risk can perhaps be best called "*discovery based.*" It goes without saying that this is by far the most common approach used in supporting experiential learning interventions. When delivered effectively, the facilitator poses artful questions that allow participants to see "their world" through a new lens. The stop, analyze, compare, consider, conclude, described earlier is overcome by providing adequate time for reflection.

Problem solving facilitation is as the name suggests. The facilitator helps the group define the problem(s) and then takes them through a series of steps aimed at solving/overcoming the problem(s). Typically those steps are (1) identify the issue; (2) agree on the success criteria; (3) draw out the barriers preventing success from being achieved; (4) agree on the steps to overcome those barriers; (5) develop a what, when, who, how, action plan.

Warrior facilitation demands maturity and experience. It takes emotional toughness to confront the team in the "heat of battle." It takes tact, timing, and know-how to take a team member aside and provide provocative feedback. To knock the team out of its complacency, to cut beyond the veneer of "going along," to dig out team members who are not committed, warrior facilitation can be very effective. Warrior facilitation is a fast track to the heart and spirit. The downside: the facilitator is taking considerable personal risk and a softer approach ruffles fewer feathers. For this reason, masterful warrior facilitators **always** contract upfront, with participants, how the session will be facilitated. Failure to do this is likely to mean that the facilitator will be perceived – especially at a senior level – as overly aggressive

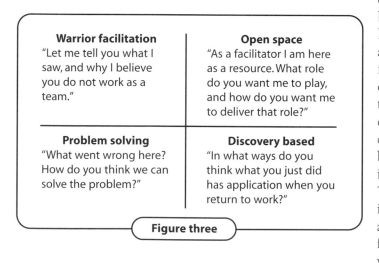

Warrior facilitation
"Let me tell you what I saw, and why I believe you do not work as a team."

Open space
"As a facilitator I am here as a resource. What role do you want me to play, and how do you want me to deliver that role?"

Problem solving
"What went wrong here? How do you think we can solve the problem?"

Discovery based
"In what ways do you think what you just did has application when you return to work?"

Figure three

and somewhat disrespectful. "Contracting" is less about asking permission than it is about seeking agreement over the best way forward. Those new to facilitation should avoid warrior facilitation. A final caution! Warrior facilitation in a culture that the facilitator does not know well is rejection waiting to happen.

Open space facilitation allows the participants to decide the style of facilitation that they feel would best serve their needs. This doesn't mean, as on one occasion observed by the author, that the first hour of a three-hour session is taken up by discussing the facilitation approach.

Organizations are poorly served by much that passes for facilitation. Facilitation is a genuine skill that can be played out in a number of different ways. There is no reason, for example, why all four approaches cannot be used in the *same* session. The message is a simple one: the facilitator is not an observer. He/she is critical to the learning experience.

Learning and change

Businesses are not philanthropic institutions. Noble as the emotions may be, few companies are in the business of personal development. Benevolence carries little weight in the capital markets. As for the undeniable duty of organizations to "give back to society" – it is a privilege limited to those who first know how to win.

Best-in-class organizations invest in learning because they know without it they cannot survive. They know that driving down cost and improving quality is dependent upon the quality of the learning available. They know that branding the learning experience is what draws outstanding talent to the organization. They know that the

> *A successful organization doesn't invest in people, it invests in its future.*

nature of the learning experience is what keeps their best people there. Those that lead such organizations know that without access to world-class learning any thoughts about being a world-class organization are pipe dreams. To strip out or to mismanage the learning process is to abandon tomorrow's possibility. A successful organization doesn't invest in people, it invests in its future.

If you are going to be asked to dance with the Red Queen first you have to know how to dance. And if she keeps introducing new steps… learn those steps or step aside. Learning is about change. To learn is to change. The speed of learning is the speed at which the organization changes.

Organizations have been dealing with this thing called change – seriously at least – for two decades or more. What have we learned? It is quite clear that what works in one place doesn't necessarily work someplace else. In like vein, we now know that change never ends. In other words, there is no such thing as a change program. We know that change has to be about the business. Change intended to apply the latest fad or technique is about ego. We know that change means giving up an assumption held in Western culture since the early days of the Industrial Revolution: the belief that people are merely a cog in the organizational machine. We know that change is about dissatisfaction with the status quo and that tension is an essential ingredient. We know that change encompasses the organization, how people are led, and the leadership of self. In fact it is mainly about self. Anyone asked to lead a change initiative and who, as a first step, does not ask, "What do I need to do differently?" is destined to fail.

We know that learning strategies that do not drive/support change are fundamentally flawed. Organizations that think they can deliver wide-scale change without excellence in

The nine steps in large-scale change

1. *Why are we in business*	2. *Pull steering team together*	3. *Build buy-in from the top team re:*
• Mission • Vision • Values • Brand	• Select key members of the top team • Work through Mission, Vision, Values, Brand, and Leadership competencies	• Mission/Vision/Values/Brand • The speed and scope of action • Leadership competencies • Assessment of key leaders
4. *Make the brand live*	5. *Shape the culture*	6. *Build buy-in from top 200*
• Story • Symbolism • Distribution channels • Measurement	• Structure • Story, symbolism • Measurement • Learning tools • Communication channels	The learning process must: • Model the "new world" • Address the head, involve the hand, engage the heart, and enrich the spirit • Change mindsets
7. *Align all the elements in the system*	8. *Drive learning deep into the organization*	9. *Figure out how fast this can be done and then do it in half the time*
• Talent acquisition • Compensation • Processes and technology	• Leadership • Coaching • Collaboration • Role specific 360° feedback	• Do it and fix it • Plan for short-term gains • Celebrate small wins

Figure four

learning would be far better to go out into the parking lot every Friday and set fire to a pile of money. It will have exactly the same effect except that it will have the benefit of being far less time-consuming. We also know that little, short of an act of God, would create excellence in learning if the organization lacks for outstanding talent in those roles that create, organize, and deliver the learning.

Figure four describes where learning fits into a broader "map" of large-scale organizational change. The model isn't presented as a way forward that fits every situation, but as a general framework that has validity from the author's own experience. Although learning is critical throughout, there are times when "how" people learn is at least as important as "what" they learn. This is perhaps best brought to life by briefly reviewing each of the steps.

1. *Why are we in business?* Any enterprise has to have a reason to exist… its raison d'être. That does not mean that the underlying driving force behind the business is unchanging. The mission describes the reason for being in business. It must also answer two other key questions: What business are we in? Who is tomorrow's customer?

   The vision describes what tomorrow's success will look and feel like. The vision is a story that describes a compelling future. In that we cannot distinguish between mental rehearsal and reality, a vision introduces people to tomorrow, today. A vibrant vision is a long way from the empty, you can't tell them apart, future-oriented goal statement many organizations refer to as their vision. A vision throws down a challenge. A vision creates an emotional tension between "what is" and "what can be." The power of a meaningful vision is found in the words of Antoine-Marie-Roger de Saint-Exupéry, the French World War II writer and pilot: "If you want to build a ship, don't drum up the men to gather wood, divide the work and give orders. Instead, teach them to yearn for the vast and endless sea."[2] A poet's lines of verse deliver an enduring truth: no dream…no passion.

   Someone once said that a river without banks is a swamp. An organization without values is a swamp. Values give primacy. Values define what is absolutely essential. Given a choice of paths, the organization's values allow the traveler to decide which one to take. Organizational values that have meaning are aligned with the personal values of those who make up the organization.

   > *A vision throws down a challenge. A vision creates an emotional tension between "what is" and "what can be."*

   The brand describes the organization's identity: the promise both specific and implied by the organization to society, to its customer, and to its employees. If "the promise" is misaligned with the mission, vision, and values, winning trust becomes an exercise in manipulation.

---

[2] *The Wisdom of the Sands.*

2. *Pulling the steering team together.* Headed by the CEO, the steering team critically examines the mission, vision, values, leadership competencies and brand. Where any of the elements described need refreshing or even reinventing, the steering team develops a first draft. The leadership competencies serve to answer a make or break question: As we move forward in pursuit of our vision what does it mean to be a leader around here? The steering team should be small and comprised of the organization's best. Ego, hidden agenda, points scoring, foot dragging and/or political expediency destroy the integrity of the team.

Four roles are essential. A visionary: a leader who can paint the picture that describes tomorrow's success. An explorer: a leader who emphasizes the commercial reality of the organization's journey. A warrior: a leader who pushes the team to act. And a navigator: a leader who creates the map(s) that links the thinking organization with the doing organization. Absence of these key capabilities severely handicaps the potential effectiveness of the team. (To read more about mastery in these roles, see Chapter Ten.)

3. *Building buy-in from the top team.* The thinking developed by the steering team must be validated by the top team. If those in key roles don't passionately embrace the mission, vision, values and brand, it is difficult to see why anyone else in the organization should. The top team also needs to build agreement around the scope of change, the speed of change, the organization's overarching leadership competencies, and the means whereby leaders at *every* level will be assessed against those competencies. Leaders need to be quickly assessed against the agreed competencies. Failure to act, a wait and see attitude, destroys trust. Talent acquisition, coaching, mentoring and marshalling the learning resources are all dependent on the quality of thinking that goes into developing the organization's leadership model.

4. *Make the brand live.* A winning brand is like an old friend. Even if you haven't met for a long time there are qualities about him/her that you know will not have changed. Indeed, within minutes it is as if you have never been apart. Brand speaks to consistency, commitment, capability, consumer care, and above all character. Character is what we draw on when the unanticipated happens. Character is hinku.

Organizations spend millions on presenting their brand in the market place and ignore the most important person in the brand war...the employee. We speak about managing from the outside-in and then toss aside an invaluable emotional bridge between the business and the market place. Step into the corporate offices of a bread company and if the employee restaurant doesn't smell of fresh bread, they are not making their brand live. Visit the reception area of a computer business and if you sign in using a pencil, they are not making the brand live. If the brand says "we care" and you don't see pictures painted by employees' children on the walls, then they are not living the brand. If the environment that the "virtual" leadership center uses to deliver its learning events isn't a visual, kinetic and auditory representation of what the organization believes in, those running the show are not making their brand live. Don't expect to hear the greatest hits of the Mormon Tabernacle Choir at the Hard Rock Café!

A winning brand is like an old friend. Even if you haven't met for a long time there are qualities about him/her that you know will not have changed.

Brand is a picture-laden story told to both established and potential customers that says, "This is who we are!" It's a story that employees also have to believe. And they can't believe it if they don't hear it!

5. *Shape the culture.* Leaders that make culture an afterthought make a grave mistake. Shaping mindsets, breaking the established patterns of play, introducing new metaphors, storytelling, challenging those who do not live the values, agreeing on what is going to be measured and how, must start as early in the change process as possible. Two other issues central to "culture" have to be folded into this work: structure (how power is distributed), and a review of the organization's communication channels. In communication – as in everything else – leaders lead by example.

6. *Buy-in from the top 200.* Clearly buy-in from the CEO and his/her team is not enough. The organization has to invite all of its important actors onto the stage. And it is not just a matter of telling. This choreography of the learning experience is as important as the content. The heart and spirit must complement the head and hand. All four are vital…all four must be part of the learning design.

The firefighting experience isn't about the fire, it's all about making what it means to be a leader come alive. Tap dancing isn't about the dance, it's about the auditory sensation of hearing teamwork in action. It's about feeling the rhythm of creative collaboration. It's about moving learning out of the head and anchoring it in the body. It's about breaking established ways to act. It's about living "the performance." It's about giving people permission to be different. It is especially about giving people permission to be different!

Leaders need to come from these sessions not just with a mental sense that this is the way forward, but with an emotional commitment to be part of making it happen. Leaders – at whatever level – who don't act, perpetuate the past. To act is to involve. To act is to challenge. To act is to reach out for new ideas. To act is to teach. To act is to coach. To act is to share positive stories. To act is to ask for feedback. To act is to be open to being coached. To act is to mentor. To act is to develop other leaders. To act is to be a positive role model by living the values. To act is to challenge those who don't. Leaders must lead!

7. *Align the elements of the system.* The mission, vision, values, brand and leadership competencies come together as the organization's genetic code. It is a blueprint for

action that must be replicated in **everything** the organization does. It is vital, for example, that change enablers such as compensation, performance management, career development, succession, and talent acquisition be a translation of that blueprint. It must also imprint (1) the sales process; (2) the way technology serves the organization; and (3) the conversations that take place between those seeking to reengineer the organization's business processes.

8. *Drive learning deep into the organization.* The learning craft displayed in gaining buy-in for the top 200 must be extended to include the total organization. Here all of the learning tools must be brought into play: action learning, simulation, e-learning, coaching, seminar, workshop, study tours…the whole artillery. The success of the learning lies not with what people know, but how they perform. Thus the single most critical outcome of every learning experience must be "What can I do differently on Monday morning?"

It is worth emphasizing one underutilized learning approach: action learning. Albert Einstein said, "I do not teach my students, but provide conditions in which they can learn." Action learning focuses on real problems, is organized in teams, and is action based…it is about change. It is about learning through doing. It is also about learning how to learn.

Based around a project defined by the team (or a number of individual projects) and sanctioned by the organization, the best action learning projects have the following characteristics:

- The steps that define the way forward should not be easy to map out ahead of time.

- The project must be important to the organization and not a "theoretical" exercise. For this reason, setting financial targets is an imperative.

- Each project needs sponsorship from the top of the organization.

- Team members should be those who are willing to challenge the status quo, who display independence and who are driven to take responsibility for their own learning.

- The best teams are those that have access to all of the mastery paths outlined in Chapter Ten.

- Team learning benefits significantly if a skilled facilitator helps draw out the ongoing learning.

The difference between action learning and more traditional project learning comes to the fore in the way the team learns together. By challenging, by testing their ideas, by sharing feelings honestly, by giving absolutely open and honest feedback, through structured reflection, and in coaching each other, the learning involved can be dramatic and lasting.

At this point, if not earlier, the organization will need to reach out and engage learning partners: consultants and educators who bring specific knowledge and skill to the learning experience. The potential value of a learning partner can be gauged by the following:

- Shared values.

- Best-in-class knowledge and experience.

- A facilitation style aligned with the needs of the situation.

- The capacity of the "partner" to reinvent what they do and how they work in line with the organization's emerging needs and culture. Few potential partners meet this need preferring, for the most part, to download what has worked elsewhere.

- Continuous stream of new ideas.

- Preparedness to work in a spirit of collaboration with the other partners, something that few consulting groups are comfortable with.

9. *Figure out how fast this can be done and do it in half the time*. Those who orchestrate the change process must model the clockspeed needed to live in a Red Queen World. Holding back, waiting until things are perfect makes you part of the problem. The name of the game is do it and fix it, but fix it fast and fix it right. The other key characteristic of success is to keep it simple. This means not just elegance of design but planning for short-term wins and celebrating those wins. People don't want to wait two years before seeing something happen. Front-line employees live in a world where the decisions they make today impact the organization next week. They expect no less from those who lead them.

Turning the world upside down

Stand at the edge of a natural cliff. Stand looking out into space, knowing that your destination, a small rock at the edge of a rapidly flowing river, lies 200 feet below. Stand, contemplating the moment when you will jump. Stand, knowing you are safe but feeling in the pit of your stomach that this may not be such a good idea. Your team urges you on. You jump. In the next instant you understand all of the emotions involved in letting go. You free-fall ten to fifteen feet. Your safety harness catches you. You belay the rest of the distance to the rock below. You have achieved the goal using only two hand signals. You are still dry and your team has won "arrows" towards a final shoot out. You are having "fun." You congratulate your colleagues in English but five or six languages are spoken in the team. You are learning what it is like to be at the edge.

A little later that same day you stand knee deep in snow being taught how to use a 30lb bow. Your teacher, a Zen Buddhist and master in the martial arts, introduces himself by handing you "an instrument of death." He teaches you to shoot, not through hand/eye coordination and sighting the target, but through feel. "You are the target," he states with a simplicity that defies argument. At the end of the day he shoots blindfolded from twice the distance. He hits the center of the target. The team is learning what it means to be best in class.

Front-line employees live in a world where the decisions they make today impact the organization next week. They expect no less from those who lead them.

The story continues...At 7.00am the next day participants are served a full dinner with all the trimmings, including wine. The world has been turned upside down. This cannot be! The team delivering the learning serves breakfast. "I cannot give you eggs, señor, I am only the waiter." Shades of Fawlty Towers or Saturday Night Live. For those attending it is yet one more "surprise."

They are forced to see the world anew. The session, accompanied by after-dinner drinks for those who want them, moves to the main room. They are into it now. The "how to" of reframing mindsets follows. To start the session, the leader (yours truly) rides into the room on a bicycle. Half an hour earlier he helped serve dinner...or was it breakfast?

Following the "breakfast" and mindset session, the organization's top human resource professional describes what it means to be a business leader. He outlines the Group's overarching leadership competencies. Those attending are seasoned leaders. Participants understand that the competencies are non-negotiable. The discussion, which lasts for the rest of the day, is keen nevertheless. Commitment without this sort of session is impossible.

The event lasts three and a half days. There are no traditional lectures. Openness, candor and honest feedback underscore all that takes place. During one session the leader responsible for strategy across the organization slowly takes his shirt off while he speaks. People are open mouthed. This is a very serious guy. No one had been warned that a striptease was part of the experience. Without breaking stride he puts on a T-shirt with the organization's values blazoned across the front. They have been given permission to be different.

The patterns of activity constantly change. Part of the time focuses on storytelling. Storytelling is used as a way to honor the past. The stories also help surface what those listening must be willing to relinquish. Some of the stories bring a tear to the eye. The storytelling is a final act in bringing the group together. Any perceived difference between the different divisions represented is by now irrelevant. True synergy lies in the heart and spirit.

During the evenings participants make a video about what it means to be a leader. The competition goes to the edge. Play is actively encouraged. Humor surfaces. Some of the offerings are hilarious. Those are the ones that win. The prize-giving ceremony on the final morning is intense. People want to win. At least half of the videos, in a playful way, make fun of the CEO. He loves it.

On the final morning participants are handed a small card that, to the uninitiated, looks exactly like a credit card. Printed on the card are the organization's vision, culture and leadership competencies. Down one side in the fashion of a credit card is a strip for signature. The cards are given out purposefully. Each leader is handed one personally. They are told that if they are committed to the direction being described they should sign the card and put it in their wallet. "The card gives you permission to confront any behavior that contradicts what we have discussed here. If the organization is not for you please return the card unsigned. We do not want you to 'quit' and stay."

As a final act, and to create a sense of drama around the reality that there is no such thing as 90% commitment, participants are invited to drive a nail into a pine board with their bare hands. They all do it. Welcome to a Red Queen World. Welcome to a world where learning and change are synonymous. Welcome to the learning edge.

What to do differently on Monday

1. Is it clear what it means to be a leader in the organization? Review the learning being enacted across the organization. Is it supported by learning as play or play as learning? Is the learning folded into compelling metaphor that brings the learning to life? As a first step, create the metaphor.

2. Does the delivery on leadership programs and events model the leadership behavior needed in the organization? Change those facilitators/tutors/professors/consultants whose style is misaligned with what leaders in the organization need to become.

3. Is there a leadership map of the organization's change journey? If not, create one. Without a map you are lost. Review the nine steps in large-scale change.

4. Does the learning enacted breathe life into the brand? Change everything to do with learning that does not reinforce the message carried by the brand. If the learning processes don't make the brand dance, ongoing investment in the marketplace that attempts to win customer loyalty is a waste of money. (See also Chapter One.)

5. The top leaders must believe. Create a learning experience that gives the top 200 people in the organization the opportunity to challenge and shape the course that the organization is charting. Part company with leaders who "leave" (don't deliver emotional buy-in) but "stay" (remain in the organization but don't live the values).

The path to mastery

Book Two

Leadership

of Others

Chapter four

Why playing with the dolphins beats swimming with the sharks

Book Two
Leadership of Others

Dan is big, gruff, and aggressive. At meetings he enjoys playing "Gotcha!" At work, it is said, one crosses him at one's peril. In life he is treated with a mixture of awe, fear, and respect. Talented, experienced and successful, on the surface at least, Dan simply devours the weaker supervisors and managers he runs across. Dan just loves eating these bass. After all, Dan is a shark.

Identify a tough job, one where the nature of the problem means "going to war with the competition" or "taking the company by the scruff of the neck" and the likelihood is the quest will be on to find a shark. Once hired, Dan, or someone much like him, is in business – and look out bass!

This is not to say that bass are helpless. Bass have a whole range of defense mechanisms. There are a lot of them, and when faced with attack they are capable of forming strongly-bonded teams. Teams that develop defensive tactics aimed primarily at warding off attack. Teams whose tactics are aimed at derisking the status quo, by describing why initiatives are destined to fail, and why adherence to rules and past precedent is essential.

Bass are not stupid. Bright, articulate, and often highly educated, bass are particularly adept at warding off attack by muddying the waters in which they swim. This is achieved through a range of well-honed tactics, but is especially effective when positioned as "It may work elsewhere, but we are different." This is a tactic that invariably starts with some variation of the phrase "If only . . ." Underpinning this tactic is not the forlorn hope that delay, abstraction or finger-pointing will end in the death of the shark. The tactic is primarily creating a vacuum of action, with the hope that the shark will move on to new and different prey. It is also a tactic which, it should be pointed out, has historically enjoyed a high degree of success.

Why not hire a shark? If the competition are acting as predators, surely a shark is demanded? On a prima facie basis there is indeed a case for a competitive, aggressive, action-oriented leader, even though he/she is likely to generate some interpersonal debris along the way.

A more critical eye, however, discerns a different sort of challenge. Businesses "managing change" are, in essence, striving to generate a degree of alignment between the organization, the way it does business, and a wide range of factors external to the business that cannot be controlled. To succeed and perhaps even survive, leaders must learn not how to manage change, but how to ride the crest of change, how to use the energy of turmoil and chaos to propel the business into the future. At a more basic level, the challenge involves two organizational imperatives. The first: responsiveness. When quality and service become order qualifiers, speed of response becomes the true basis of differentiation.

The second imperative: organizational learning, a topic that has received a great deal of press but is poorly understood. Without an inherent ability within the body of the organization to learn from experience, develop a heightened capacity to act, and reframe established practice at critical points on the journey, responsiveness is destined to remain little more than a twinkle in the sales representative's eye.

Much as one might peel an onion, beneath responsiveness and learning lies individual and team mindsets: the way each of us sees the world. Our assumptions about work and organizational success frame our behavior. To survive in the white water most of us have entered demands courage, skill and, above all else, an ability to appraise and respond appropriately to the world emerging around us. Survival means we all have to change.

The openness to do things differently and think about the world differently should, however, not be thought of as a linear process. It is much more like climbing a mountain. A base camp is established, and only once the base has been consolidated can the next camp be set up and supplied. Equally important, in an organizational sense, assumptions have to "shift" at each stage of the journey. Responsiveness and its handmaiden, learning, represent a journey, not a destination: a journey covering three Territories, (T1, T2, T3); a journey dependent upon effective leadership; a journey punctuated by discontinuity. *(See Figure five.)*

The journey is not for everyone. Those operating within a commodity-type market, where the value proposition is exclusively drawn out of the price of the product or service, often decide that a T1 organization is an appropriate fit with a business model predicated on being the low cost producer. This does not mean that all T1 businesses eschew empowerment and employee involvement. Through an ethos of continuous improvement and employee development, a number of leaders have pushed the T1 model to the very edge of what is possible ("enlightened" T1). Many organizations (e.g., Toyota) have evolved what can best be described as a "parallel structure" – organization forms where, although the day-to-day work gives little opportunity for initiative (T1), time is set aside to allow front-line teams to redesign the business process that contains the work being undertaken (T2).

The ultimate arbiter of organizational effectiveness is the marketplace. Put more succinctly, customers have a habit of voting with their feet.

Other business sectors, however, have little choice but to move to an organization form dominated by a T2 way to be. The ultimate arbiter of organizational effectiveness is the marketplace. Put more succinctly, customers have a habit of voting with their feet. The reality: where the value proposition is based on customer intimacy, where the business model is one that means the product or service must be continuously reinvented, or where intellectual capital is the ultimate arbiter of market success, it is unlikely that a T1 mindset will deliver the organizational agility needed.

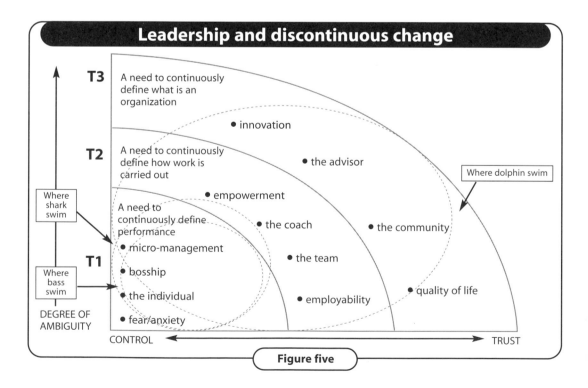

Figure five

If the journey being described is not a journey every organization will want to complete, it is equally not a journey all leaders are capable of charting. Sharks thrive in a world of aggression, survival and one-on-one competitiveness. Like sharks, bass are uncomfortable when swimming outside of familiar waters. (*See Figure five.*)

Enter the dolphin. Elegant, highly intelligent, fast and adaptive, the dolphin represents a powerful metaphor for a new leadership form, capable of moving across all three territories. The dolphin seeks collaboration, looks to improve effectiveness by impacting the total system and seeks to expand rather than exploit its natural boundaries. The difference is most clearly identified in how a dolphin creates a powerbase. A shark reaches for the organization chart and emphasizes title and formal authority. The dolphin asks new questions.

Apart from speed and elegance, the dolphin has a number of natural assets that makes it the true master of its environment. Comfortable swimming in harmony with others, it can communicate across all three territories. Sharks, on the other hand, see other species as natural prey and are, above all, programmed to attack. Weakness and helplessness are a shark's lifeblood. Dolphins respond to signals of helplessness in an empathetic and caring way. As for bass, they, for the most part, spend their lives complaining that things are not as they used to be.

In years past it was relatively easy to distinguish between species. The clear crystal water of unimpeded progress made the markings of each easy to spot. Today's turmoil has created numerous underwater eddies and has made the waters murkier. As a result, one needs to look beyond the immediate and the superficial and observe behavior and language. (*See Figure six.*)

Sharks are always on the move. Egocentric in their actions, they like to fill the room with the energy of their own voice. This is their hunting song. When listening, they do so not in a supportive, empathetic way, but with the self-interest of the hunter. Shark language is punctuated by the use of war-like and combative stories and metaphors which, in turn, are emphasized by the short stabbing or chopping motion of the swordsman delivering the kill.

When things get tough, bass are easy to spot. They are the ones hiding in a hole in the coral. When a challenge is presented they ask, "Why me?" The bass is the one who comes into your office to complain but who personally doesn't want to do anything about the problem. Bass resolve conflict by appearing to go along. When the economy is bad, bass ask for contracts that guarantee security of employment. When the economy is good, bass start a chorus of why things are about to get worse.

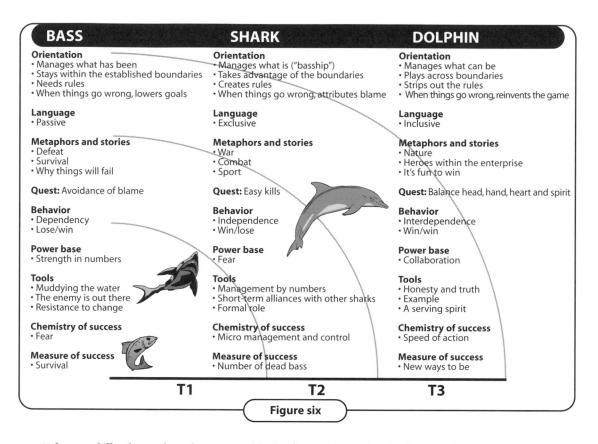

BASS	SHARK	DOLPHIN
Orientation	**Orientation**	**Orientation**
• Manages what has been	• Manages what is ("basship")	• Manages what can be
• Stays within the established boundaries	• Takes advantage of the boundaries	• Plays across boundaries
• Needs rules	• Creates rules	• Strips out the rules
• When things go wrong, lowers goals	• When things go wrong, attributes blame	• When things go wrong, reinvents the game
Language	**Language**	**Language**
• Passive	• Exclusive	• Inclusive
Metaphors and stories	**Metaphors and stories**	**Metaphors and stories**
• Defeat	• War	• Nature
• Survival	• Combat	• Heroes within the enterprise
• Why things will fail	• Sport	• It's fun to win
Quest: Avoidance of blame	**Quest:** Easy kills	**Quest:** Balance head, hand, heart and spirit
Behavior	**Behavior**	**Behavior**
• Dependency	• Independence	• Interdependence
• Lose/win	• Win/lose	• Win/win
Power base	**Power base**	**Power base**
• Strength in numbers	• Fear	• Collaboration
Tools	**Tools**	**Tools**
• Muddying the water	• Management by numbers	• Honesty and truth
• The enemy is out there	• Short-term alliances with other sharks	• Example
• Resistance to change	• Formal role	• A serving spirit
Chemistry of success	**Chemistry of success**	**Chemistry of success**
• Fear	• Micro management and control	• Speed of action
Measure of success	**Measure of success**	**Measure of success**
• Survival	• Number of dead bass	• New ways to be
T1	**T2**	**T3**

Figure six

Whereas difficulty with ambiguity and lack of vision limit the shark to a relatively small part of the pool, the dolphin is quickly identifiable by its ability to traverse the water available - even expand the size of the pool. The language of the dolphin is expansive. The dolphin uses words to paint a picture not merely of the way things are, but the way things can be. The dolphin's metaphors are more global in nature, often encompassing humor and stories from nature to reframe perceptions. The dolphin, unlike the bass, is also comfortable swimming at any depth and, with one thrust from its powerful tail can move from the surface to the bottom of the pool and be equally comfortable – be it organizational level, dealing with concepts, or involvement in operations.

The dolphin is perceptive and, with exceptional powers of hearing, is quick to identify other species. The bass, hardwired to survive, has a sensory system that alerts it to the presence of other bass. Equally, it is highly attuned kinetically to the physical and emotional noise emitted by the shark. The shark operates from instinct. If in doubt, the shark attacks. If a bass is the object of such an attack, the shark may well back off. After all, the bass can be always be devoured at will. Such seemingly generous behavior builds intense loyalty from the bass. This symbiotic relationship feeds the fear of the bass and nurtures the feelings of superiority inherent to the shark. For the bass, the interaction fuels self-doubt and a heightened fear of the unknown. For the shark, the behavior of the bass is yet more proof that hierarchy, rules and "basship" are essential ingredients in the leadership mix.

If the shark's attack uncovers a dolphin, it is only because the dolphin chooses not to swim to those parts of the pool where the shark will not venture. Like a judo expert, the dolphin uses the shark's energy against itself. The dolphin responds to problems by reframing the context; creating strategic opportunities; encouraging diversity; and welcoming constructive conflict as an opportunity to generate new ideas. In short, dolphins confuse and frustrate the heck out of a shark, and a frustrated shark is not a happy shark.

Can sharks or bass become dolphins? Each of us has elements of dolphin behavior built into our psyche. It takes courage, however, to tear down the protective barricade of the functional organization. It takes courage to swim out into uncharted waters, to approach established problems in new ways, and to respond to aggression with innovation and subtlety.

Orchestrating such a shift is nevertheless what lies ahead. Sharks will have to be tempted to operate against their natural instincts. They will have to learn how to add heart and spirit to their head and hand view of the world. Bass will have to be encouraged to take risks. Fortunately, the dolphin is a wonderful navigator.

In that 90% of major organizational change initiatives fail, there is clearly a need for a dolphin-like leadership. Nowhere was this more apparent than in the litany of failed process-reengineering initiatives. Orchestrated by "sharks" whose sole goal was to reduce cost regardless of the human impact, the outcome was predictable: resistance, game-playing and the destruction of value. Interventions that should have been aimed at reducing process complexity and creating expanded roles were responsible, instead, for destroying the organization's last vestiges of heart and spirit. Put simply, when the sharks acted like sharks the bass, in turn, were forced to act like bass.

Tomorrow's leaders will have the added burden of having to learn how to succeed in a wide range of organizational forms.

Organizations must nurture the dolphin they currently have, give them the whole length of the pool to swim in (process), and understand that aggression and criticism are as natural to the shark as timidity is to the bass.

History indicates that the quality of leadership available and business success are synonymous. Tomorrow's leaders will have the added burden of having to learn how to succeed in a wide range of organizational forms. With a key supplier the relationship may very well be in line with a T1 way to be. Where a strategic alliance comes to the fore the leadership needed is likely to be congruent with assumptions framed by T2. To encourage breakthrough thinking, a T3 mindset is appropriate. Moreover, tomorrow's leader will have to be comfortable as the boss on one team, a coach with another, and advisor to a third.

The way forward represents a leadership journey punctuated by plateaus of consolidation, and energized by successive reframing of assumptions about the world around us. Leadership development must, in particular, equip those involved such that they have the "bandwidth" needed to be successful in different territories.

Many traditional aggressive managers and supervisors who have been described as sharks are not equipped to make the journey – their instincts lie elsewhere. Similarly, others who have been termed "bass" will be too intimidated by what lies ahead and too fearful to swim away from the shark. A new leadership form is demanded and leadership development actions needed to encourage the growth of such executives. This new leadership is best described as "the way of the dolphin." Adaptive, combative when necessary, dolphins (through creative collaboration) can and do – if no other course is open – kill sharks.

What to do differently on Monday

1. The T1, T2, T3 model is a simple but meaningful way to outline to frontline employees the cultural change journey being enacted. Does a similar map of the journey exist in your organization? No map…no journey! Initiate such a map, a conceptual framework that allows employees at every level to discuss, understand, and challenge the way forward.

2. Do the processes that support the best use of human capital (e.g. succession) reflect the need to build leaders who can operate concurrently in T1, T2 and T3? If not, work to bring that fundamental realization about.

3. Is there alignment between the emerging value proposition and the organization's dominant learning platform (T1, T2, T3)? For example, a service ethos that demands agility, freedom to act and team support will not, and cannot, thrive in a T1 culture. Make culture and competitiveness part of the same conversation.

4. There is a good deal of talk in the business press about the value of building a "coaching culture." Is it understood that systemically anchoring coaching in a T1 culture is akin to entering a carthorse in the Derby? Make "setting the context" an essential part of your coaching work.

5. Challenge the bass. Confront the sharks. Cheer on the dolphins.

Note: This Chapter is based on an article originally published by MCB UP Ltd, Burdett, John O. "Why Playing with the Dolphin Beats Swimming with the Sharks", Journal of Managerial Psychology, Vol 8, No 5

Chapter five

Leaders are storytellers

Book Two

Leadership of Others

More is less

There is a blight upon the land. The paradox of the information age is that the smarter we get, the dumber we act. Its most apparent manifestation is that modern man is drowning in a sea of cultural "pollution." Pervasive advertising, useless e-mail, an endless stream of sexual imagery, movie and television violence, an impenetrable wall of simplistic music, unsolicited marketing overtures…all make "turning off and tuning out" a mental health imperative.

The Internet is transforming English into a jargon-dominated lingua franca demanding little more than the literacy of a ten-year-old.

More, ultimately, means less. In sacrificing something as simple as silence we have turned our backs on an important part of that which in earlier times nourished us. Moreover, in a world where the irrelevant has been proclaimed "important" – the sexual adventures of an incumbent President warrants dramatically more airtime than a quantum increase in child poverty, and being a celebrity carries with it the assumption that the individual must have something of value to say – it should come as no surprise that apathy rules. The outcome: a twenty-first century citizenry whose time-span of attention is defined by a McDonald's menu, Much Music, the news sound byte, and the 30-second commercial. And if your pizza isn't ready in six minutes you get it free!

Faster food isn't better food. The vocabulary of the modern teenager is half of that enjoyed by those who grew up in the sixties. The Internet is transforming English into a jargon-dominated lingua franca demanding little more than the literacy of a ten-year-old. Even executives no longer have the time or the energy to read. The problem: there is an indelible link between language and behavior…there is a direct correlation between an individual's ability to access language and his or her ability to think and act differently. The reality: when we look back ten years from now, today's rate of change will appear pedestrian. What we are currently living through is tomorrow's *good old days!*

Leadership is about followship, so the implications for those aspiring to take the helm are profound. And at the risk of repeating a point already made…more communication is absolutely not the answer. Shop-floor terminals, groupware, Intranets, distance learning strategies, broadband, wireless technology and palm devices speak volumes as to speed and accessibility. They remain mute and disinterested partners, however, when it comes to the quality of the message being delivered. We continue to invest in ways that appeal to the head and address the hand while remaining seemingly oblivious to the real leadership challenge – the need to engage the heart and enrich the spirit. The paradox is that the more channels we create, the less communication we have!

Story: part of our heritage

Enter stage left the power of story. Man's earliest organizational forms were created, nurtured, and indeed were transformed, through story. Story is not only as old as man but is a fundamental building block of our cultural and social heritage. When we sat around the campfire after a day of running down a Woolly Mammoth we relived that experience through the power of story. And what we learned we passed on to the next generation through story. Our very identity, the inner sense of who we are, is rooted in an oral tradition. Greek literature as in *The Iliad* and *The Odyssey*, and epic poetry such as *The Kalevala* and *Beowulf* would not exist were it not for our tradition in storytelling. Similarly, Aboriginal Dreamtime and Native American methodology make powerful statements as to the link between story and culture. Simply put, history tells us that leaders were and are, of necessity, *storytellers*.

Presentation and instruction in their many guises are the medium through which power is exercised. Much of what passes for corporate communication needs to be kicked, pushed, and manipulated, before it moves (slowly) through pre-existing channels. As a result, persuasion and other forms of coercive communication seldom outlive the problem or issue that created their need. By comparison, an effective story has a life and energy of its own. A good story creates its own path. It does so because story collapses the traditional boundary between sender and receiver…we deliver information, but we *share* a story. Instruction and directive invariably frame the audience as the problem. Story evokes options that allow the listener to identify with the solution. A directive is exclusive. A story is inclusive. New rules breed resistance. A story builds community.

When traditional forms of communication attempt to weave together ideas, humor, imagination, challenge, and/or self-critique, the transition is apparent. Like a badly-fitting toupee, the join is clear to all. In story, however, the subtleties of language blend together so that the story can be retold many times without the original resonance and/or energy being lost. Moreover, at each telling a new sense of the possible, a new and deeper insight into the story's underlying emotional weave is available to both the listener *and the storyteller*.

To be a leader is to learn how not to be an actor

Here it is important to distinguish between story and anecdote. Story is rooted in authenticity, and is delivered out of a desire to serve. A story is a strand of oral DNA plucked from the storyteller's personal journey. To share a story is to bring something of oneself to the listener. Story speaks to each individual in a unique way. Anecdote, although of value in reinforcing the message, is ultimately about enhancing the performance. At a superficial level they may sound the same, but to the listener the difference is dramatic. Anecdotes are a tool of the actor. Story is born of the spirit and delivered from the heart. In story the

A story is a strand of oral DNA plucked from the storyteller's personal journey

person that we are is fully present. Story expresses what the leader deeply believes in. Stories are drawn out of truth. To be a leader is to learn how not to be an actor. It is not about playing or becoming the role, it is about being the role.

Stories bring to life that which would otherwise be mundane. A well-crafted story weaves Head, Hand, Heart, and Spirit together in a way that makes the message not only easy to understand, but delivers a vivid memory that long outlives more traditional forms of communication. Stories are a uniquely powerful medium because they touch the listener emotionally. Stories make the listener part of the experience. A good story is literally unforgettable. It is no accident that when any of us attend a seminar, workshop or training event, what we remember (often years later), is not the content of the session but the stories the presenter used to drive a point home. Moreover, in retrieving that story we access, without even knowing we are doing so, the underlying learning involved.

Storytelling and change

Organizational change initiatives that fail to recognize the power of story are bankrupt before they begin. Stories can be part of the solution or part of the problem. Stories often recycle yesterday's failures. Stories can fan the flames of cynicism. A negative story acts like an anchor. And ancient though an anchor may be, when lowered, when buried in the mud, it can prevent even the most technically advanced vessel from leaving port. Where then lies the way forward? Let me share a story.

I have a small lawn both at the front and at the rear of my home. They do not cover a large area but they do provide a pleasing view from the house. That was until they became infested with dandelions (a small but virile weed that, when in bloom, has yellow flowers).

The problem seemed simple enough. After all, the chemical industry has spent billions of research dollars on exactly this problem. The solution was not to be found quite so easily, however. Chemicals certainly reduced the problem but somehow the pesky weeds seemed to survive.

It was then that I happened to listen to a local radio show that took calls from listeners concerned about lawn care. And yes, a little old lady had exactly the same problem ... she couldn't get rid of her dandelions.

The expert quickly discounted the use of pesticides. He said, "You won't be able to get rid of the dandelions by trying to get rid of the dandelions." "Absolutely!" I said to myself. "The way to get rid of your dandelions," he continued, "is to make the rest of the grass so robust, so aggressive, so strong that it strangles the villains to death."

The message, of course, was clear. You can't get rid of negative stories by trying to get rid of negative stories. Those responsible for charting a new organizational direction must provide the tools, the opportunity and the means whereby positive stories are so robust, so aggressive, so strong and so pervasive that they strangle out of existence those negative stories that would, in other circumstances, have remained firmly anchored in the organization's cultural mud.

The building blocks of story

The very best stories are simple to understand; are drawn out of truth; describe real people and real events; hold meaning for the listener; are believable; are something that the listener can relate to; use language that the listener is comfortable with; describe, at least in part, a positive outcome; and contain a new question. Although often told in a way that makes the listener discover elements for him or herself, a good story is made up of four central building blocks:

1. What is the story about? What history does the listener need to know? What issue, dilemma or opportunity does the story address? Who are the key players in the story? *This part of the story speaks to the head.*

2. What was the hero/heroine's journey? What tragedy, dilemma or problem did the main character(s) overcome? What opportunity was created or seized upon? *This part of the story addresses the hand.*

3. At each critical juncture in the story how did those involved feel? What is the drama? Who learned what? *This part of the story engages the heart.*

4. What happened? What did those involved find out about themselves? Who else gained and how? What did those involved share? *This part of the story enriches the spirit.*

Leaders collect stories

Successful leaders not only tell stories, they collect them. Story helps others better understand what is important. Values are conveyed and made manifest not by a framed statement but through story. Critical incidents are brought to life through story. Encouraging the employee to share his or her story is central to the act of coaching. Stories convey culture. Stories give texture to symbolism. Stories evoke new mental maps. Complex ideas are often best conveyed through story. Stories give rebirth to the child within. Those who formed today's great religions, Christ, the Buddha and Mohammed, were all storytellers. History tells us that leaders who achieved sweeping and lasting social change, Winston Churchill, Gandhi, Martin Luther King Jr., were able to do so, in part, because of their mastery of storytelling. Great leaders tell stories that live in perpetuity.

The increasingly important role of story is evident in every aspect of the leadership experience. A recruitment process built around the belief that "When money talks, talent walks" reaps its own rewards: zero loyalty, constant churn, and a dash for the exit when the share options are no longer above water. Talented people are drawn to an organization for a variety of reasons: the financial package, personal growth, the organization's reputation, freedom to act, location, the role played by leadership development and the markets served. Moving to a new organization may appear to be ruled by the head but, like all major life changing events, has far more to do with listening to the heart. Logic appeals to the head. Stories touch people's hearts. When it comes to talent acquisition, organizations don't compete... stories do.

Story is a critical element in the learning process. In writing down our own story, in keeping a journal, in writing articles or business reports that capture our experience we are entering into a rich process of reflection. Reflection is the key to self-discovery. Without reflection new pathways soon become overgrown, new patterns become lost and new ideas become overwhelmed by that which has been. Those who do not reflect fully on what has worked and what hasn't are destined to repeat past mistakes, become a captive of the latest trend, and easy prey for those who offer the quick fix. Without the capacity to build on past reflection, new levels of uncertainty represent not opportunity, but a vortex of confusion from which there is no escape. Leaders who do not create time for reflection are building into their persona an inherent redundancy that leads inevitably to derailment.

To mentor is to share one's own story. A good story shares not only what happened but the twists and turns along the way and the underlying motives involved. Through story the listener gets to peek behind the curtain and connect with the hero's/heroine's vulnerability. Through story the listener is being made aware of the mentor's approach to decision-making, propensity to take risk and professional/personal values. In listening to the mentor the

> *To lead without accessing the power of story is to carry a quiver full of arrows but to have left the bow at home.*

individual being mentored is finessed into asking of him/herself: "Is this how I would have approached the problem? Were I faced with a similar situation how would I react? Was there a better way?" By sharing the "lived experience" of a more seasoned executive, the listener is forced to explore his or her own mindset, filters, biases and beliefs. It is this, when added to the opportunity for reflection, that makes mentoring such a unique and powerful learning experience.

Conclusion

To lead without accessing the power of story is to carry a quiver full of arrows but to have left the bow at home. The typical employee is overwhelmed, confused and burnt-out by the weight of communication he or she has to deal with as part of everyday life. Because of this, flaccid, uni-dimensional, self-serving communication that seeks to instruct and/or control is destined to become yet one more piece of unneeded and unheeded clutter. Story is a piece of the communication puzzle that no successful leader can afford to ignore. When confronted with the impossible, when asked a question that has no simple answer, when standing in front of an audience whose support is vital, the most valuable thing a leader can do is to start off his or her comments with the phrase… "Let me share a story."

What to do differently on Monday

1. Listen attentively to the stories that move around and across the organization. Do the stories that seem to have a life of their own support the organization's journey … or make success less likely? Collect those stories from within the organization that support the organization's vision. Share positive stories every opportunity you get. Make your aim to be a great storyteller. Practice, practice, practice.

2. Learn from those who already display mastery. Go out of your way to spend time with others in the organization who are great storytellers. Listen to the rhythm and the simplicity of their stories. Watch how storytelling breathes life into what would otherwise be a bland communication. Make storytelling an integral part of leadership development. Make sure everyone involved in the talent acquisition process knows and can share the company's story in an engaging way. It's not organizations that compete…it's stories!

3. Make storytelling part of how people share best practice on your team. Start each meeting with one rich story. Make storytelling part of your coaching capability. When you coach someone for the first time open the conversation by asking the coachee to share his/her story.

4. Have members of the team share their own story. You will be amazed how little people really know about each other and how the simple act of sharing who they really are can break down barriers. When someone is new to the team, similarly, have him/her share his/her story as a way to move into the team.

5. Find at least one opportunity on Monday to start a sentence with the words: *Let me share a story.* Remember, great leaders are great storytellers.

Chapter six

Talent acquisition: where have all the leaders gone?

Book Two
Leadership of Others

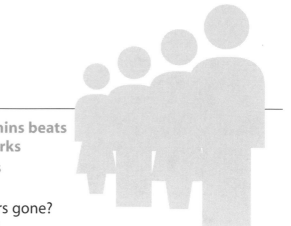

Management Review, the American Management Association Journal, in describing the single most critical issue facing business at the dawn of a new century, made the following assertion: "It's executive talent. Or rather the lack of it. For at least the next five decades, companies around the world will be scrambling to find qualified managers and executives." And yes, you read it right. *Fifty years!*

The collapse of many of the dot-com organizations – although clearly throwing many technical specialists on the market – has done little to resolve what for many organizations has emerged as their biggest single challenge…attracting and retaining leaders of the highest caliber.

Faced with a leadership shortfall one might reasonably wonder what our business schools have been doing for the past three decades. What of the billions of dollars spent by organizations on executive development? And let us not forget the virtual avalanche of books available on leadership. Does anyone read them?

Central to the problem is that leadership is more than a set of techniques. Leaders who make a lasting difference know they are competing for people's dreams. Leaders who leave a rich heritage are those who have discovered that the assets that matter most lie within. As for executive development … much of the effort, energy and time aimed at developing talent to deliver performance is predicated on a business model that has its origins in a leadership approach that thrived at the beginning of the *last* century.

Then, of course, there are all those books. The disappointing reality: millions sold…few read. As for the "best sellers," they rarely offer more – by way of language, content and ideas

– than can be digested on the flight between London and Paris. The dilemma: in a world where a good deal of the learning demanded is literally difficult, it is important to differentiate between *keep it simple* (the elegant design of a Formula One race car where absolutely anything that adds unnecessarily to the weight or hinders speed has been, and continues to be, stripped away) and *making it simplistic* (complex ideas reduced to the lowest common denominator). Perhaps it's enough to say that the old adage, "Leaders are readers" is truer today than ever.

And forget the quick fix! Golden handcuffs, signing bonuses, slicker videos, attendance at more job fairs, more outsourcing, swapping executives with other organizations, setting up research facilities in remote locations, and accessing ever more recruitment websites may well be positive actions. But such actions, in isolation, do little to address what are, invariably, deep-rooted systemic problems.

As with much in life, the challenge isn't forging agreement over the nature of the problem, but deciding what to do about it. The first obvious conclusion is that organizations have little choice other than to strive for excellence in their talent acquisition initiatives. What this means in practical terms is that issues hitherto thought to belong to Human Resources – the leadership process, culture, branding, competencies, organization "fit" and executive integration – are rightfully critical measures of the success of the top team. Those who think otherwise should remember that with many leadership positions – and especially when going outside – the organization is literally betting its future on the individual selected.

Where did all the leaders go?

Finding and keeping talent can no longer be labeled as merely "important." As the AMA suggests, it has become the single most impactful issue facing the twenty-first century organization. Lack of resources and/or lack of leading edge thinking when it comes to talent acquisition and the organization is inevitably finessed into a position where the selection process is based not on who fits, but who is available. Hello, mediocrity!

The reasons that lie behind the current leadership shortfall differ somewhat from industry to industry but, taken overall, have five distinct origins:

1. *Clockspeed.* The speed at which markets are changing combined with the drive from the capital markets for short-term results have demolished traditional notions of strategic planning. As a result, today's successful leaders are not those who know how to sit back and "plan for the future." Today's successful leaders are those who make tomorrow's ability to compete integral to how those *at every level in the organization* think and act.

2. *The temporary nature of competitive advantage.* Market advantage is temporary. Today's successful leaders possess and stimulate a mindset where continuously challenging the organization's value proposition becomes a way of life; they understand that today's solutions are of necessity redundant; and they have the courage, when demanded, to let go of even that upon which the organization is founded.

3. *Cultural bandwidth.* The merger/acquisition trail blazed over the past decade means that few organizations can be said to have a single culture. The growth of international business merely exacerbates this dilemma. Today's successful leaders are those who have a proven ability to reach into their bag of experience and apply and support what works best, be it formal hierarchy, a team-based empowered approach, or the creation of an e-learning supported, virtual community.

4. *The coaching imperative.* Business leaders have finally discovered that the real competitive leverage comes not from innovation, technology, or even financial strength, but from the depth and ability of its leadership talent pool. Thus, the leader who cannot find the time or who lacks the capacity to coach is ultimately an organizational liability. Similarly, leaders who do not know how, or lack the will, to develop their leadership talent are destroying value in a way that can only be described as a fundamental breach of their fiduciary responsibility.

5. *The learning context.* The final reason for the lack of leadership talent lies not so much with how the world of work has changed, but in how those served with supporting the modern organization have failed to keep abreast of the emerging demands. MBA students leave the institution that trained them with a deep understanding of financial ratios but with little or no understanding of how to shape the culture of the struggling business they have just joined. A case study aimed at sharpening how people think may be interesting, informative and even stimulating, but is ultimately a very poor substitute for knowing how to hire talent or lead a change initiative. Put more broadly, as a society we have invested heavily in three generations of "leaders" who know virtually everything there is to know about the head and the hand but who have been seduced into believing (through omission and example) that the heart and spirit don't really matter.

It is not enough to talk glibly about leadership; organizations must define specifically what it means to be a leader (in their organization). Lack of such direction…there is a clear shortfall in stewardship from the top. Lack of agreement to the direction being forged… there is a need for richer and more meaningful dialogue. Lack of buy-in…the organization's leadership problems are systemic, deep-rooted and urgent.

In a steady-state world, "to manage" was acceptable, even lauded. In a world where the marketplace is constantly redefining success, the capacity to reinvent what is possible is the only game in town. Where did the leaders go? Those whose raison d'être is to improve the status quo are never in short supply. Conversely, those with the ability to move the organization into new territory have never been easy to find. The dilemma: no modern organization can survive, let alone thrive, with a philosophy of incremental change and/or the belief that in yesterday's questions lie tomorrow's solutions.

Key questions:

1. Is what it means to be a leader in your organization clearly defined?

2. Is that leadership definition based on the reality that there is no such thing as sustainable competitive advantage?

3. Are those who seem to want to follow their own leadership agenda brought to task?

4. Is there clear and unambiguous support for the heart and spirit dimension of the leadership process? Note: this is not to suggest that the head and hand are not equally important.

5. Do leaders clearly understand that they need a range of interventions, structures and leadership approaches in their "tool bag"? Is the organization's leadership development built around this key assumption?

Defining the emerging culture

A good deal has already been said about culture. Even so, to discuss talent acquisition without reference to culture would be to figuratively attempt to build a house without first constructing the foundation. There is merit, therefore, in reiterating key points made in earlier chapters:

• Few (if any) organizations can be said to have a single homogeneous culture. Indeed, any reference to culture in an era of the "fragmented organization," must encompass suppliers, partners, and a whole host of people who, although not in the traditional sense employed by the business, create value for the customer.

• Culture is a container for diversity. Too much diversity and chaos reigns. Too little, and innovation is strangled at birth. Assumptions that culture is about sameness are, at best, naïve.

- A culture that allows people to be what they are capable of becoming must build on people's personal values.

- Culture captures not simply what needs to be done, but *how* things get done. As a result, the message contained in "the brand", when combined with the opportunity provided by technology to create new communication cartilage, has a dramatic impact on what people give primacy to.

- Culture is anchored in the organization's history, use of symbolism, ritual, mindsets, metaphors, stories and language.

- Culture is, in part, an outcome of what gets measured.

- Culture is about how power is distributed. Changing the way people make decisions is to change the culture. Creating new opportunity for creative collaboration is to change the culture.

- Culture is never static. To ignore culture is to act as if the chainsaw screaming at full power in the next room doesn't exist.

- Culture is expressed in how people learn.

Confusion as to what is meant by culture can be found in the belief that in large-scale change, culture can be left to the end. If you can toss a stone into a pond without causing a ripple, there may be merit in that point of view.

Like teamwork, culture is a term that conveys much but all too often delivers little. Process reengineering, merger, acquisition and, indeed, talent acquisition all suffer from this ill. Need that be the case? Does culture have to be relegated to the lowest rung on the ladder of understanding? Must culture always be a vague, ephemeral, hard-to-grasp dimension of the recruitment and leadership development process?

The answer: absolutely not! Leading edge organizations use well-honed tools to enable them to better understand both the current and the emerging culture. A better understanding of the culture, in turn, means that the thinking around the key leadership roles is based on a rich description of what tomorrow's success sounds like, feels like and looks like. To act from a speculative, blurred, nebulous view of the future is to set forth in a howling gale without knowing how deep the water is and where the rocks lie.

To lead is to translate the dream into language and imagery that make the dream both accessible and compelling: the vision. But having a vision isn't enough. To succeed, to build a platform for talent acquisition and growth, organizations must be able to make the emerging culture live in people's hearts. For the dream to live, culture has to become more than a vague, fleeting and shadowy concept. Culture must represent a pragmatic, measurable and hands-on aspect of every leader's conversation about what it means to deliver lasting change.

Key questions:

1. When people in the organization speak of culture are they all talking about the same thing? If the answer is yes, how do you know?

2. Does the organization have a successful track record of quickly merging cultures (as in merger and/or acquisition)? If not, why not? When a new business is acquired are the tools in place to *measure* culture, and thus define cultural disconnects?

3. Do external partners who support the organization's change initiatives (consultants, executive search partners) bring a deep understanding of culture to the table?

4. How is a hard-edged measure of cultural fit integrated into the selection process? How do those who meet potential talent describe the organization's culture? Are they consistent? Is the language and imagery used such that the dialogue around culture encompasses front-line employees?

5. Is it understood that no organization has one culture, and that leadership development experiences represent a poor investment if they don't equip leaders to succeed in a range of different cultures? Is leadership development aimed at creating and delivering success in *tomorrow's* organization?

Branding the leadership experience

A simple but fundamental statement is "You can't hire 'em if you can't find 'em." Over the *past fifty years* we have been slowly drawn into a mindset that presents leadership as being largely of the head and hand. Strategy, systems, processes, technology, reengineering and the illusion of the quick fix have all been deemed to be the difference that makes a difference. Meanwhile downsizing, merger and acquisition, cost reduction and a mercenary approach to information technology have destroyed much that, in past times, represented a sense that the organization was "our place." Ford's willingness to wire up its 350,000

What engages people is not the boxes on the organization chart, but the chance to play in the white space that surrounds them.

member workforce by offering each of them a computer, a printer and Internet access for $5 a month, may be the harbinger of a revitalized approach to building community. The heart and spirit has been torn out of the "modern" organization. People yearn for a rich learning experience, challenge, work that has meaning, commitment, openness, honesty, trust, truth, authenticity, belonging, a sense of being part of something that reaches beyond the profit motive, and a belief that the rewards of success are shared fairly. Put simply: what is missing is often a reason to stay!

What excites young and not so young leaders is the opportunity to grow. What keeps talent is not the size of the compensation package, but the scope of the challenge. What engages people is not the boxes on the organization chart, but the chance to play in the white space that surrounds them. Organizations that have put leadership development on the back burner are metaphorically starving the corporate body of oxygen. And guess what... the body will eventually die! Here we speak not just of leading programs and courses, but building on an underlying ethos that says, "To work here is to become everything I am capable of being." The new game is informality, risk, stretch, self-development and feedback. Lots and lots of feedback.

Having a better mousetrap is not enough, however. People will beat on your door only if they are made *aware* you offer something special. Even then, be it through website or personal contact, there is a very small window of opportunity to convey the worth of listening to your story. The new reality: best-in-class organizations spend considerable time and energy in *branding the leadership experience*.

Key questions:

1. Does your company website convey the quality of the leadership experience?

2. Did last year's annual report capture the excitement of being a leader in your organization?

3. Do you take the time and trouble to share the "leadership experience" through storytelling, whether internally or through magazines, periodicals and newspapers?

4. Are young leaders trained and encouraged to speak about their work experience on external courses and seminars? Are those who achieve a level of excellence in this regard financially rewarded?

5. Are leadership programs more of the same old fare, or are people screaming to attend? Are they exciting? Do they take people to the edge? Does each event represent a true emotional and unforgettable experience? Does the learning strike a balance between the head, the hand, the heart and the spirit? Does the change being orchestrated display a deep understanding of experiential/action learning?

6. Do external partners (e.g., executive search organizations and major consulting firms) play a key role in *measuring* and giving feedback on the effectiveness of your leadership branding?

7. Are leaders rewarded for developing talent? Are those who coach and develop others recognized, or do they suffer the fate of so many talented leaders... the better they are, the more people they lose to impoverished parts of the organization?

Generic versus specific competencies

Two lessons emerge for those organizations that lead the way when it comes to recruiting leaders. The first: hiring for the role in question using replacement logic is an opportunity lost. The second: establishing what leadership success will look like in behavioral terms is an imperative. The first insight speaks for itself. The second is a more subtle issue.

It goes without saying that a list of tasks and responsibilities – useful as they may be – is a poor substitute for actually being able to describe the behaviors aligned with success in the role in question. This was first realized in World War II when selecting officers for unusual or dangerous assignments. What emerged was an approach to selection based on what British Army psychologists referred to as a set of "competencies."

"Competency," and all that the term implies, has received a tremendous amount of attention in the past decade. Indeed, rare is the organization that does not have at the center of its leadership development agenda a series of statements to describe "leadership success." Recruitment, mentoring, coaching, 360° feedback, succession and promotion, for example, are all processes that build on the relevance, quality and meaning of the organization's leadership competencies.

Organizations use different ways to describe what is meant by the term competency. For some, competency describes a set of minimum standards. For others, competency is the means to capture what is meant by "excellence." A third group applies competency to mean a set of underlying attributes such as knowledge, skill, values and self-image. McClelland (1993) describes competencies as "basic personal characteristics that are determining factors for acting successfully in a job or situation." A useful working definition is that competencies describe a set of traits or attributes that, when bundled together, distinguish an outstanding candidate from a "middle of the road performer." Lack of a definition of what is meant by the term "competency" is but one area where organizations stumble.

Here we come to the subtlety described earlier. Organizations, in using competencies, have become used to, and in some respects wedded to, a single set of *generic* competencies that span the total organization. "Keep it simple!" is the cry. If culture is about everyone being the same, a single set of umbrella competencies makes perfect sense.

Generic competencies can indeed be an invaluable piece of the puzzle in the recruitment process (i.e., is this individual a good fit with the organization overall?). Experience from best-in-class organizations, however, suggests that it is a mistake to use generic competencies *in isolation* to describe success. The generic leadership profile should be complemented by a set of competencies developed specifically for the role being filled. Reliance on generic competencies exclusively would appear to be based on several somewhat dangerous assumptions:

- *The organization has one unified and homogeneous culture where the degree of freedom and opportunity to act is the same.* Taken to a logical conclusion, this statement suggests that terms such as "drive for results" and 'teamwork" would mean the same for the leader of the unionized manufacturing business in Detroit that the company wants to sell as it does for an executive working for the same business running a start-up, web-based, marketing enterprise in China.

- *Leaders are literally interchangeable.* In today's ever more complex business environment few would agree with this: it would lead to the unlikely scenario that the CIO of ABC Company in New York could easily head up the same organization's biotech business in India.

- *All of our businesses are at the same stage of evolution.* The more pragmatic view would be some of our businesses are mature, some are at a start-up stage, and some are going through rapid growth while others need to be turned around. Experience suggests that a leader who succeeds in one type of business (mature) may not succeed in a business with similar products and technology at a different stage of development (turnaround).

- *All of the teams for which we are recruiting have a similar balance.* A contrary view would be that hiring someone to lead a strong team with seasoned performers is an entirely different challenge than hiring someone who will encounter a weak team filled with inexperienced team members.

- *It doesn't really matter who you report to.* The opposing view: the hiring executive based in another country, who can only visit the location infrequently, must seek different qualities than does the executive whose direct support team is at the same location.

The suggestions around competencies are not presented with the intent to diminish the value of generic competencies. It is not a matter of either/or; they describe success in general terms. Organizations would be well advised, as a first step, to ensure that candidates are matched with the generic (macro) competencies. Fit, however, is not limited to alignment with the organization but with the demands of the emerging role and this, in turn, means taking the time to develop role specific (micro) competencies.

Key questions:

1. Is there agreement within the organization as to what is meant by the term "competency"?

2. Is the selection/interview process built on a well-thought-through set of generic *and* role-specific competencies?

3. Do those competencies balance the head, the hand, the heart and the spirit?

4. Does the language framed by the competencies match the language of leadership demanded in the *emerging* culture?

5. Is performance and developmental coaching aligned with role-specific and meaningful competencies?

6. Are those competencies and the language used regularly "refreshed" to meet the changing business environment?

7. Are 360° feedback sessions based on competencies that are fine-tuned to reflect the challenges and problems faced by a specific role?

8. Does the succession process balance both the generic and role-specific competencies? Is the succession work a once-a-year exercise or a real-time database that influences all aspects of talent acquisition?

Fit is everything

Imagine the following. Let's call the executive in question "John." In the scene being envisioned, his challenge is to determine the worth to the organization of a potential million-dollar investment. Indeed, this is the fifth such review John has undertaken in the past six months. Little or no training…well, let's not dwell on that. Lack of preparation…does it really matter? That the organization's needs are poorly defined…who has the time? The fact that almost half of past investments appear not to have worked out…it's too late to worry now. Oh! and in case we should forget, the poorer John is at assessing this type of asset…the more of them he will be asked to do. Heck, if he's bad to the point of being dysfunctional…he will spend virtually all of his time on this work.

Tongue-in-cheek as the above example may be, for all but a few organizations, this is the reality. Audit a typical organization on either side of the Atlantic and the unassailable evidence is that the talent acquisition process is, at best, a hit and miss affair. Disagree? Heard the following recently? "Culture is important but not something you can really get at." "Sam, pull out the job description we used the last time we hired for this position." "Role specific competencies!?…we don't have time for that, and besides, I know what I'm looking for." "If that executive search company we hired calls tell them I can let them have 45 minutes." "Get back to the candidate and tell her I can see her in three weeks." "Have I been trained and coached in how to interview? Well, I took a program, let me see, nine years ago that I seem to remember was pretty good. Anyway, I have been interviewing for years." If these statements sound even remotely familiar, there is work to be done. More to the point, if the comments are not too far removed from something that could come out of your own mouth… *you* may be part of the problem.

Nothing is more important than fit. There is no investment a company makes that is more value-laden and at the same time more potentially damaging than the act of hiring for a leadership position. And, in today's organization, more and more people are needed who will display leadership. Fit is not a magical elixir. Fit is a discipline. Fit is about doing the work. It is about describing what it is that the organization needs to do to create value for tomorrow's customer and, with that understanding in mind, defining *specifically* what tomorrow's culture needs to be. It is about developing a role definition that is aligned with tomorrow's success. And here the operative word is tomorrow! *Replacing* someone is another way of saying "quick fix." Hiring that is drawn out of assumptions describing what we need to do well *today* is a problem being given birth.

Fit is about spreading a wide net, illuminating dark corners and looking for candidates in places that redefine what is possible. Fit is about knowing what success looks like. It is about capturing the critical competencies and then boring down to determine if the candidate can deliver. It is not about hiring the "best" candidate… it is about hiring the *right* candidate. Fit lies with those who display commitment. Fit is found in a will to win. Fit is about looking for those who are optimistic because optimism is self-fulfilling. Fit means hiring team players. Fit is enacted when all of those involved in the selection process keep setting the bar higher.

Evaluating fit lies initially with the head: does the candidate have the intellectual horsepower to be successful? Is he or she a visionary? Does he or she display helicopter thinking? The head must be complemented by the hand: does the candidate have the skills? Does he or she know how to do the work? Fit must encompass the head and the hand but fit is also about the heart and spirit. Fit is about balance. The heart speaks of a passion to learn and the capability to

> *As a rule of thumb, organizations are advised to hire for heart and spirit and train, as needed, around the head and hand.*

develop others. The spirit is about identity, community and connection. Does the leader display a serving spirit? Can he or she bring a sense of meaning to the direction being charted? Is the journey about him or her or about the success of the team? When things get tough, what inner resources can this individual call upon? To what is he or she loyal?

Although absolutely essential, leaders rarely fail because they lack head and hand capability. These qualities are relatively easy to identify and shortfalls can often be addressed. Conversely, leaders cannot succeed if the heart and spirit is found wanting. Issues such as lack of authenticity, avoidance of conflict, a distrust of openness, a lack of optimism, fear of failure, a low propensity for risk, and a need for control, not only destroy the very fabric of the organization but are very difficult to fix. As a rule of thumb, organizations are advised to hire for heart and spirit and train, as needed, around the head and hand. This is not to imply that organizations should therefore skew their ongoing leadership development towards the head and the hand. Arguably, the contrary is the case.

It is difficult to explore fit without reference to the ubiquitous interview. The interview can be highly effective. It is, after all, a critical tool in solving the problem of fit. In practice though, the reality often lies elsewhere. A rapier in the hands of the expert, the interview, as wielded by the majority of those who consider it to be part of their mandate, more often than not delivers the "killing power" of a wet newspaper. This lack of effectiveness lies in lack of training, poor preparation, too little time allocated to the interview, lack of synergy between interviewers and inadequacy of information garnered. An example of the latter can be found in the biographical interview – an approach historically much beloved by executive search professionals – which yields little that isn't already captured by the resume.

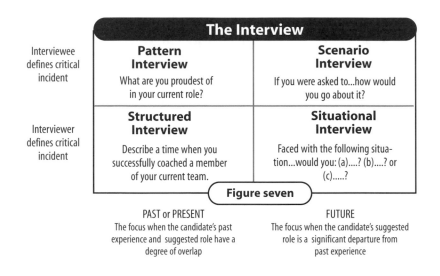

The single greatest indictment of those who interview – and even professional interviewers fall into this trap – is over reliance on a single tried and trusted approach. *Figure seven* outlines four interview approaches (there are, of course, a number of others). Successful interviewing is a little like fly-fishing: success depends on an ability to read the conditions and know what species you are after. This doesn't mean that the four techniques listed stand in isolation. In the hands of a real pro they become blended into a single, seamless, purposeful conversation. Before moving on, there is value in describing the four approaches outlined:

I. *The structured interview:* the interviewer explores the candidate's fit against each of the key competencies. Questions (focusing on critical incidents) are drawn directly out of the competencies in question with little attempt to mask the competency being sought (e.g. "Tell me about a time you successfully *coached* one of your subordinates.") Value: highly effective when in the hands of a master interviewer and relatively easy to conduct. Limitation: because of the way that the questions are asked, the competencies are "telegraphed" to the interviewee. What the pros do: plan the questions ahead of time and dig, dig, dig.

> *Successful interviewing is a little like fly-fishing: success depends on an ability to read the conditions and know what species you are after.*

II. *The pattern interview:* the interviewer asks the candidate to identify the critical incident (e.g. "Tell me your proudest accomplishments over the past six months.") By digging into the what, why, how and who gained, and with the pre-determined competency in mind, the skilled interviewer builds an understanding of the candidate's patterns of behavior. By subtle questioning the interviewer is able to draw out the knowledge needed to evaluate the candidate against each competency. Value: the absence of a direct sight line between question and competency makes it very difficult for the candidate to know specifically what the interviewer seeks. As a result, a good deal of the game-playing is set aside and the interviewee finds far less opportunity to run his/her "tape." Limitation: not easy to do. What the pros do: plan ahead of time and then play multi-media video frames in their head that capture all the richness of the question and then, based on the interviewee's answer, put the candidate in the action.

III. *Situational interviewing:* developed originally by Professor Gary Latham of the University of Toronto, this methodology assumes that the behavior of high performers can be translated into an "ideal" selection template. Step one is to identify critical "incidents." Each incident, in turn, represents a typical dilemma facing those in the same or similar role to the one being interviewed for (e.g., a critical piece of software unexpectedly displays a major problem the day before launch). Step two involves designing (and validating) at least three plausible responses to each dilemma by asking high performers how they actually do respond to such a situation. Candidates are presented with both the future dilemmas and range of possible answers. Successful candidates are the ones whose answers match the behavior of the organization's performance champions. Although used mostly with what are referred to as "multiple occupancy roles," situational interviewing can be highly effective with executive positions. It is invaluable in situations such as a plant start-up. Value: high legal validity. Limitation: time of preparation. What the pros do: ask each question totally without emotion. In this way the interviewer avoids giving the candidate any sense of what the ideal response should be.

IV. *Scenario interviewing:* presents future scenarios to the candidate and asks how he or she would approach and/or solve the problem (e.g., " Business A is faced with the following problems....if you were to take charge what would you do?). The interviewer is looking for not just the what, but the why, how and who will gain. Value: the critical competencies remain somewhat masked. Limitation: how someone says he or she will act isn't always how they do act. What the pros do: research what a best-in-class leader in the culture in question would do when faced with the scenario outlined.

No one concerned with the issue of fit should ignore self-selection. Fit is ultimately about honesty. It is about sharing what's good about the organization, what is bad and, if necessary, what is downright ugly. An informed cry along the lines of "This role/organization is not for me" is cause for celebration.

Finally, without taking the time to determine fit… be prepared to smile, accept your own personal version of *Groundhog Day* and shout out a hearty "hello" as you greet your mistakes every morning – every morning – every morning.

Key questions:

1. Does every high-potential employee spend time in a role that has as one of its key responsibilities organization-wide recruitment?

2. Is there at least one person – it could be an external resource – whose sole role is to continuously enrich the recruitment process? Note: the role in question needs to be delivered by a real professional and be hands-on. It would, of course, encompass such things as sitting in on interviews and coaching leaders in the selection of external resources. The return on such an investment potentially amounts to many times the initial cost.

3. When was the last time you benchmarked the recruitment process, and not just against the best in the industry? What changes did you make?

4. Is there a forum where the most creative people in the organization get together to explore new places to look for talent? Is the mindset behind that creative effort an assumption that nowhere in the world is too remote and no field of endeavor too far removed?

5. Has the organization fully explored the opportunity provided by Internet recruitment? Does the organization use video conferencing? Is there a company-specific recruitment website? Is the site linked to other key websites including suppliers and customers? Does the site include well-written articles, recruitment tips, games, quizzes, book reviews, and other reasons for the casual visitor to want to return? Does the website tell the organization's story in a compelling way?

6. Is there a spirit of excellence at the center of the recruitment process that allows for past precedent and practice to be set aside when a uniquely capable candidate is discovered? Does that include making an offer even though there may be no immediate position available? Is the offer made fast?

7. Are external resources such as search partners on a retainer to keep them continually on the lookout for talent, regardless of any formal openings that exist? Are such partners integrated into the company culture so they have a deep understanding of *tomorrow's* needs?

8. Do the executive search organizations you are working with bring to the table (1) true expertise in the area of culture? (2) a process that enables them to succinctly define the role? (3) the tools needed to evaluate the team needs? (4) the capacity to define the competencies for the role? (5) the interview processes/skills necessary to match each candidate against the agreed competencies?

9. How does the organization respond to resumes and inquiries for employment that are not a good fit? Is it a matter of a standard letter, or is each response seen as an opportunity to shape the organization's reputation in the marketplace?

10. Do you have a process that establishes standards for, and measures the quality and effectiveness of, the recruitment process? Is the process subject to the level of process improvement, redesign and innovation as are other key processes in the organization? If not, why not?

11. What steps are in place to discover (1) why people stay with the organization and, (2) why those who leave do so? Are tenacious, *independent*, external resources used on this work?

New role, new reality

Executive integration conjures up images of a raging river. On one bank lies the past and on the other, the future. Although the turf may look similar, each side of the river supports its own unique ecology. The river – a metaphor for the speed of change – bubbles and sings from the energy of the white water that covers its surface. A deafening roar greets our executive as he/she approaches the edge. The symphony of noise makes communication difficult. Confusion and delay mean that the noise will get ever louder. Success, in the form of fit and the ability to meet the expectations of those who have paid for the journey, lies on the other side. However, the spray from the water makes the far bank difficult to bring into sharp focus. One moment it is there and the next it is lost. The executive we are watching is lucky. The organization has laid out a series of stepping-stones to make the journey easier. Indeed this executive is truly fortunate, for on the far bank a mentor stands both giving encouragement and identifying those stones that need to be approached with caution. Both are aware that although one slip is unlikely to be fatal, several will result in exhaustion. The clock is running. Attempts to leap over a stone are fraught with risk. Surprisingly few organizations have taken the trouble to put any stepping-stones in place and even fewer have trained lifeguards on hand. It should come as no surprise, therefore, that even expert swimmers lose heart and give way to the forces that lie ready to sweep them away.

Considering the failure rate of mergers and/or acquisitions and the poor track record of organizations delivering large-scale organizational change, a reasonable benchmark is that at least 40% of those moving into a new role do not make it to dry ground. The number of CEOs that drown is certainly higher. The reasons for this waste of talent lie in several areas: failure to describe the role appropriately, a tired or inexact way of building the competency profile and a general lack of attention to the selection/interview process.

High on any list of reasons why leaders fail when they move into a new role is that after an enthusiastic welcome, he or she is left to swim for it. And even if he or she cries out for help the answer from the far bank is likely to be little more than a faint, "We would like to help you, but…." The dilemma: critical "stepping-stones" such as letting go, getting to grips with the new culture, building a high-performance team, reaching out for a mentor, understanding the organization's strategic drivers, defining the role, recontracting for performance excellence, coaching and building a personal development plan, are often ignored by organizations. Not supporting key integration steps is to court failure and invite disillusionment.

Lack of talent is somewhat like a broken wheel on a wagon: it won't fix itself, and if left untended long enough the structure is destined to collapse.

The most likely scenario: after an enthusiastic start the new leader is thrust into the fray with little thought as to the support that would most benefit him/her. The new warrior is thrown into the battle without first being handed the weapons he or she needs to win the fight. The inevitable response: the new leader reverts back to that which he or she knows; he or she is inevitably drawn to that which worked in an earlier organization.

Once the bloom is off the rose, once the new leader displays a vulnerability, not only does his or her self-confidence suffer but all the naysayers, cynics and those who were overlooked for the position are only too pleased to say "I told you so." The ensuing downward cycle is self-fulfilling. Even those who merely stumble are apt to make an early decision that this is not the organization for them. The reality: how a leader enters the organization makes a significant impact on his or her emotional commitment to the business. Put more succinctly, *those who don't land, don't stay!*

To spend tens of thousands of dollars or more on recruitment and then pitch the new leader into the organization in the hope that he or she will somehow figure it out is an act that defies logic. Internal promotion, a move to a different country, acquisition and/or merger, all deliver the same message…you're on your own! Organizations that fix this issue will be taking a major step in delivering on their implied promise of support to a new leader. In doing so they will also be setting the stage for leadership retention.

Key questions:

1. Has your organization attempted to calculate the cost of mismanaging the integration process – speed of performance delivery, the impact on motivation, lost reputation in the marketplace, increased leadership churn?

2. Does your executive search partner embrace the integration process as part of their offering? If not, why not?

3. Does the organization have a well-honed set of tools that those moving into a new role can access? Do those tools define leadership as being limited to the head and hand or do they support insight into heart and spirit issues? At a minimum, does the integration process fast track the new executive through: (1) how to let go of past ways to act; (2) coming to terms with the new culture; (3) evaluating the effectiveness of the new team; (4) understanding what drives the business; (5) reaching out to a mentor; (6) defining the new role; and (7) contracting for performance success?

4. To what extent are those in key leadership roles skilled in supporting and coaching those moving into a new role? Realizing that this is a major leadership issue, what would it take to make them successful in this regard?

5. Is new-hire mentoring a highly regarded capability? Is reverse mentoring – young professionals working with more seasoned leaders in areas such as information technology – aggressively sponsored? What would it take to make mentoring live in the organization?

* * * * *

Lack of talent is somewhat like a broken wheel on a wagon: it won't fix itself, and if left untended long enough the structure is destined to collapse. The problem: even the screech of tortured metal all too easily becomes just one more discordant element of background noise.

It matters for naught that the organization has spent thousands of hours on its strategy. The latest technology and even access to unlimited funds are of little value if, central to the way the organization conducts its business, there is not the means to find, attract and retain outstanding talent. Plato said that you could learn more about a man by watching him play for an hour than in a year of conversation. The acid test of the twenty-first century organization is to be found, not in the many superficial ways that have evolved to measure effectiveness, but in the way it identifies and develops its future leaders. The arenas outlined do not spell out excellence…they merely define what is happening on the field. Moreover, they describe not the ideal, but the *absolute minimum* it will take to stay in the game.

What to do differently on Monday

1. Make defining the emerging culture central to the talent acquisition process.

2. Work to brand the leadership process.

3. Insist that role specific competencies support **every** hire or promotion decision.

4. Become skilled in behavioral interviewing.

5. Make sure that every new hire is given the tools to integrate him/herself into the organization[1].

[1] See the author's best-selling book *New Role, New Reality*. For more details go to www.orxestra.com.

Chapter seven

Coaching: challenging the motivated, not motivating the challenged

Book Two
Leadership of Others

Coaching is in! Business magazines, consulting brochures, executive programs, and in-house leadership development workshops all provide evidence of the lemming-like rush to turn the leader into a "coach."

The potential value of coaching is difficult to argue with. Speed, leadership bandwidth, the need in a retention-conscious world for talented performers to be given the space to deliver, and an emphasis on business process (and with it the unbundling of hierarchy), all mitigate against a "power over" mindset.

The longest journey a man makes is the one from the head (knowledge) to the heart (acknowledgement).

Discourse is not doing. Demand is not the same as delivery. And leadership predicated on "power to" is little more than a disconnected dream unless those in key roles: (1) let go of the misplaced feelings of comfort provided by micro-management; (2) reinvent how they personally learn; (3) as Gandhi so elegantly suggested, become the change being proposed; and (4) insofar as coaching is concerned, embark on a personal journey of inner discovery. To paraphrase the Oglala Sioux: the longest journey a man makes is the one from the head (knowledge) to the heart (acknowledgement).

What is coaching?

What is coaching, and in what way does it differ from its kissing cousins, mentoring and counseling?

If there are two people in the room and one of them has been asked to turn over his/her car keys, we are describing a need for counseling. For alcohol abuse substitute chronic absenteeism, anger management, depression and/or any other form of addictive, aberrant or abusive behavior. Counseling is the domain of a trained professional.

Mentoring, meanwhile, can be characterized as a seasoned performer sharing his/her story with a less experienced employee, to accelerate the latter through the experience curve. A good mentor helps his/her partner discover the holes in the road *before* the latter falls into one of them.

Mentor was tutor to Odysseus' son Telemachus. In the Middle Ages, in the relationship between master and apprentice, "mentoring" became synonymous with excellence in the "trades." Five hundred years later mentoring is still about discovering the right path. Or put another way, don't expect to become at one with your own potential without a mentor.

A successful mentor is not always someone whose experience is defined by the silver trapped in the bristles of a hairbrush. Reverse mentoring – as in a young employee mentoring a senior executive in information technology – has given mentoring new meaning. In a world where change is a constant, the most effective mentor is someone who has himself/herself recently charted the turbulent waters into which the person being mentored is about to plunge. Experience even two or three years past can be stale and largely indigestible fare.

There are four distinct faces to coaching. Confusing them gives rise to many of the problems organizations face in making coaching an integral dimension of the leadership process. They differ in the following way:

- Performance coaching focuses on the *current role* and is exclusively about improving *business performance*. "Performance," in this case, means not merely exceeding that achieved in the past, or working on what others might suggest needs to be fixed. To coach is to move to the next plateau. To coach is to enable the employee to reinvent what is possible. To coach is to create new business opportunity. The organization's vision, values and leadership competencies, as well as the team's stretch goals, set the context for performance coaching. ***Performance coaching is the prerogative of the team leader.*** Exceptions to that rule include coaching input from peers and subordinates, a situation where the team leader lives in a different part of the world to the individual being coached, and/or where the person being coached is the CEO and/or owner and who, in practice, has no immediate team leader.

- Developmental coaching focuses on a new, greatly expanded or *future role*. Developmental coaching builds on the employee's vision, learning style, passion, drive to succeed, identity, and personal path to mastery. Developmental coaching is often enriched when a third party – human resource professional or external consultant – complements the role of the team leader.

- "In-the-moment" coaching describes the *opportunity* that exists in the numerous short conversations that punctuate a leader's day. To coach is to recognize the "teachable moment." In-the-moment coaching also embraces the opportunity to give positive feedback conveyed by attentiveness, gesture, tone, signal and, where appropriate, silence. In-the-moment coaching is the responsibility of all those who describe themselves as a leader.

- Coaching in how to coach is the most challenging dimension of the coaching experience. It also delivers the highest return on investment. It is tough for most leaders to deliver because, when asked, few can actually describe the source of their coaching success. Putting feelings, intuition, flair and insight into words is, of course, never easy. Those who do have this capability represent a priceless asset to any organization. Using external resources to support coaching in how to coach is a smart investment.

What is coaching? It is everything described…and more. In his autobiography[1] Quincy Jones suggests that musical arrangement is like painting. "The final product is a beautiful thing to hear, a tapestry of different colors and textures and densities, but the meat and guts of arranging is sweatshop work, a blend of experience, architecture, soul and science. You're literally tearing fears, observations, harmonies, and rhythms down to their essence and building them back up to support and re-create the song." It would be hard to find a more apt description of coaching at its very best.

It is important that each and every employee feels connected to the organization's journey, that the role involves personal stretch, and that work-life balance is front and center. If the coaching does not at the same time *improve the business*, however, it is for naught. There is only one reason a business should invest in coaching: to improve business performance. Here lies a paradox: it is only through the singer that the coach can influence the song. Famed Julliard violin teacher, Dorothy Delay, who numbered amongst her students Itzhak Perlman, Midori and Sarah Chang, attributed much of her success to the motto, "Teach the student, not the subject."

The coaching gene

Is coaching an esoteric process that only a handful of leaders can aspire to mastery in? A pragmatic view suggests that after tens of thousands of years of social evolution – which up until 4000 years ago was exclusively hunter-gatherer – modern man to survive, of necessity,

---

[1] *Q. The Autobiography of Quincy Jones. Page 99*

had to have a highly active coaching gene as part of his/her survival kit. It is a point of view that leads one to the belief that coaching, like its first cousin, teamwork, is less something to be learned than it is an inherent capability that lies waiting to be rediscovered. In *The Wizard of Oz*, the Tin Man was looking for a heart, the Lion was distraught because he didn't have courage and the Scarecrow wanted a brain. In their quest for wholeness what they learned was that the answer didn't lie *out there* but was an integral part of *who they were*; a dormant but vital part of their inner-self that lay waiting to be discovered *within*.

Those who travel the yellow brick road of coaching likewise are likely to find that their own personal mastery is far more about *being* than it is about *becoming*; it is far more about *letting go* of that which gets in the way than it is about *acquiring new stuff*. Or as Lao-Tzu said, "To attain knowledge, add things every day. To attain wisdom, remove things every day."

The road traveled comes with a map marked "coaching is not about the coach." To coach is to serve. Coaching draws on the head, involves the hand, and engages the heart but when all else is stripped away… is rooted in the spirit. Coaching can only truly come to life if it flows from a serving spirit. In the late nineteenth century Britain's two greatest Prime Ministers were William Gladstone and Benjamin Disraeli. It was said that when he walked into a room everyone knew immediately that Gladstone was the most important person in that room. By comparison, when Disraeli walked into the room each individual there knew immediately that *he/she* was the most important person in the room. No prizes for guessing who would have made the better coach.

> *In coaching as in life, the person who assumes the worst is rarely disappointed.*

To coach is to be authentic. The coach who asks for passion but who him/herself lacks passion is engaged in an act marked by redundancy of purpose. The coach who seeks to orchestrate learning but who is resistant to input from others is destroying value. The coach who overreacts to well-intended criticism is handicapping the value of his/her own feedback. The coach who espouses the need for change but continues to do the same things or new things in the same old way is the organizational equivalent of an overweight salesman selling the latest diet plan.

In coaching as in life, the person who assumes the worst is rarely disappointed. To coach is to be an optimist. It was Harry Truman who said, "A pessimist is one who makes difficulties of his opportunities and an optimist is one who makes opportunities of his difficulties." To coach is to understand the term "self-fulfilling prophesy."

Coaching works best when the coach and the coachee *have perceived parity of power.* This does not mean that only a CEO can coach a CEO. Parity of power contains four key elements: speed of thought; cultural compatibility; the "I've been there" component; and the use of language. Matching an employee who has blazing speed of thought with a coach whose ability to think through ideas and concepts is best described as pedestrian, is unlikely to be a sound mandate for success. Similarly, a Japanese executive who will demand time to build a relationship is unlikely to feel comfortable with a coach whose style and approach is dominated by robust and early confrontation. The "I've been there" element is no less important. A coach who has limited international experience offers little to an executive whose mandate is global, and whose need to act transcends cultural boundaries.

Language is the most crucial of the elements intrinsic to parity of power. The coach who cannot introduce, explore, and challenge new metaphors is a total misfit for the coachee who can and does. The coach who fails to surface and reframe meta-language (broad generalizations that lack specific content…"I need to be a better communicator") leaves much of the potential on the table. The coach who lacks a rich repertoire of conceptual models may offer something to those faced with transactional change (doing the same things better), but his/her value diminishes significantly when transitional change (a major step change, but we have reasonable time) is being tabled. Where transformational change (sweeping change, now!) is demanded, a coach who lacks the capacity to shape the conversation so that new ways to see the world emerge would have to be adjudged a liability.

Coaching is about challenging the motivated, not motivating the challenged

No high performance athlete would consider competing at the highest level without a world-class coach. The team that aims for the championship is severely handicapped if it lacks someone to take them to the next level. Flawed though sports may be as a metaphor for business, the leader who wants to deliver his/her best game should remember that even Tiger Woods needs his coach, Butch Harman.

Few business leaders, when asked to look back six months, can point to a personal coaching conversation that has had lasting impact. Few executives believe that their own immediate leader is an outstanding coach. Even fewer have been effectively (if at all) trained in how to coach. We talk of world-class performance, the mission describes the need to be Number One and yet, in the same moment, we assume that leaders drawing only on gut feel, osmosis, and the belief that it will turn out okay on the day, will be able to make it happen.

The shortfall is not one of want. Shaping the story, holding up a critical mirror through which to view established practice, breakthrough thinking, developing cultural reach, dealing with increased clockspeed, connectivity, new business models, personal feedback, the challenge of a new role, and the need for reflection are just a few of the reasons leaders give for valuing the contribution of a coach.

The shortfall is not one of capability and/or motivation. Supported by a coach who knows how to coach, the majority of leaders quickly tap into their own personal coaching gene. Moreover, when given access to the right tools, many of those same leaders attain a level of coaching mastery. You don't need to persuade an eagle that it was born to fly, and you don't need to persuade a leader who brings heart and spirit to his/her role of the need to coach.

The shortfall is not one of opportunity. In a Red Queen World, in a world where competitive advantage is fleeting, leaders are faced with an abundance of possibility. Coaching opportunities can be found in planning sessions, sales calls, someone new into his/her role, conversations around performance, changes in the competitive landscape, feedback following a key initiative, adjustment in the balance of the team, recalibration of clockspeed in the market place, missed targets, cost reduction, unanticipated success, organization change, or new partnerships. What limits coaching in organizations isn't the challenge at hand. What holds leaders back is the absence of effective role models. What limits possibility is that leaders allocate so much time to fixing problems (and feel needed in doing so) that they rarely have time to explore new ways to act.

When leaders are asked why they don't spend more time coaching the typical response is, "I don't have the time." When informed that truly outstanding leaders spend as much as 60% of the time coaching, the body language is one of incredulity. Asking those leaders who do invest a considerable part of their day coaching how he/she finds the time the answer is, "I create the opportunity to spend a considerable part of my day coaching simply because I spend a considerable part of my day coaching."

Leaders spend far more time coaching than they realize. The problem: much of that time is spent "coaching" the wrong employees. Who gets coached? More often than not it's the person who is stuck, the person who is drawing complaints, the individual who missed agreed targets. We hear and respond to the squeaky wheel.

This "remedial coaching" can be characterized in three ways. Firstly, we spend valuable time on individuals who neither live the values nor produce results, when what we should really do is transfer them to the competition! Secondly, some of the issues we attempt to address through coaching are really the province of a skilled counseling professional. The third, most problematic concern is that by investing a considerable amount of time in those whose performance we are only likely to marginally impact we ignore our most valuable resource, our champions...those who both live the values and deliver results.

We ignore our champions because they can be counted on, because they deliver. Put more simply, our champions don't seem to need coaching. Big mistake! Time spent in coaching a champion yields a several-fold return on investment even when compared with a middle-of-the-road employee. The real issue is that champions need to be coached. They want to be stretched. They want to feel that they are working at the edge of their capability. They want to feel that they are on a fast track. Ignore your champions and it will be they, and not the "squeaky wheels," that join the competition.

The value of a hired gun

Is the use of a third party coach a good idea? Clearly, those delivering the service will be quick to answer YES! They will be equally quick to point out their successes. The case for external coaching goes like this. Retaining high performance talent is getting ever more difficult. Many executives don't know how to coach. Executives are too busy to give the quality time needed to coach. An external coach can build a level of trust and get at issues to which the "boss" is denied access. An external coach is free of the politics of leadership, and thus can be truly honest and truly open. The financial case is equally appealing. Leaders are in very short supply. Replacing a leader who fails can run into the tens, if not hundreds, of thousands of dollars. Improving the performance of a key leader by only 5% or 10% makes a lasting difference that far outweighs the cost of bringing in a coach. Persuasive? Yes! Convincing? Not entirely!

The buyer's rationale: based on publicity that originates in the world of sports, the act of coaching is invariably portrayed as demanding a talent that lies somewhere between miracle worker and prophet. This myth has so entered our psyche that it has led many a business leader to throw his/her hands up and say, "Coaching is clearly too difficult for me to do well. Find me an expert!"

Even assuming that the external coach is someone who has the talent to make a difference, hiring an external coach raises a number of important concerns. Here one needs to again distinguish between performance and developmental coaching. The case for utilizing an external resource for developmental coaching is relatively easy to make. The factors that mitigate *against* using an external coaching for performance coaching are perhaps even clearer:

1. Leadership cannot be delegated. Leadership is not a sometime activity. It is not a fringe pursuit, and it is not something that can or should be outsourced. Performance coaching is the very essence of leadership. To lead is to coach. Introducing a third party into the performance equation dramatically changes – and not necessarily for the better – what

it means to be a leader. The use of an external coach is an explicit communication to younger leaders that (1) either leadership and coaching are somehow separate activities, or (2) in the range of priorities that a leader is faced with, coaching for improved performance ranks pretty far down the list.

2. Leaders who cannot coach around improved business performance are, to put it mildly, poor leaders. The remedy lies not in asking an external coach to bridge the gap, but coaching leaders in how to coach. The former perpetuates and even exacerbates the problem; the latter builds for the future.

3. The performance management process must be made to work. The modern organization spends a high percentage of its total resources seeking ways to motivate and retain its star performers. At the center of that activity lies the ongoing performance management process. The most viable part of this process, the glue that makes it work, is the coaching discussion. By separating coaching from issues such as goal setting and compensation, the organization is stripping the heart and spirit out of the performance management process.

4. Performance alignment is a leadership imperative. Change is an ever-present issue in today's business environment. Change isn't like painting a house, where you do it and forget about it. Change is continuous. Central to the issue of change is alignment, and the sharp end of alignment is found in day-to-day performance; everything else is mere rhetoric. Moreover, alignment isn't periodic. Like change, alignment is an everyday occurrence. Alignment is rooted in an ongoing need for leaders to "connect the dots" between mission, vision, values, team goals, and performance. Adding a third party to the performance equation not only takes the leader out of the play, but also runs the real risk of making the alignment challenge more difficult.

The single most important issue facing organizations is lack of leadership. It is understandable for those at the helm to support the development of leaders by bringing additional resources into play. What makes less sense is to introduce processes that shift even part of the accountability for performance to a third party. Today's business, and the challenges that go with it, demands that the performance conversation takes place between those whose shared accountability is to face down the competition day in, day out.

The coaching conversation

It is right to describe the coaching discussion as a conversation. A *conversation* because, although mutual respect is the start of it, and shared learning has always to be part of it, trust lies at the heart of it. A *conversation* because at its best *both* the coachee and the coach come away from a successful coaching exchange with a heightened awareness of self.

Coaching is a conversation with a purpose. It is also a conversation marked by a quality best described as "tough empathy." The best coaching conversations are rarely an entirely comfortable experience. Learning takes place at the edge of our comfort zone. To coach is to take the employee to the edge. To coach is to challenge. To coach is to confront. To coach is to ask questions that penetrate the employee's ego. To coach is to break through shallowness. To coach is to enable the coachee to see the business challenge from a new perspective. As for empathy, to coach is *to care*. To coach is to care enough to want to see the problem/opportunity through the employee's eyes.

To coach is to shine a light in the dark space between how an employee sees him/herself and how others perceive him/her. To coach is to understand that change may be supported by logic and persuasion but is ultimately rooted in emotion. Coaching is thus about truth. Partial truth, and half-truth, and truth that's sanitized to make the conversation less uncomfortable, are disrespectful and lacking in integrity. This doesn't mean that the coach uses truth in the fashion of a woodsman swinging an axe. Truth that has its origins in anger, truth used to wound, truth as way to manipulate or divide, is obscene. Truth that comes from the heart is an act of service. And does the employee understand the difference? Every time!

Truth is always relative. The coach in understanding this, prefaces feedback that might be perceived as negative with terms such as "I think," "My perception is," "From my standpoint." Leaving room for the employee to disagree builds a platform for dialogue and ownership. Language that presents the coach's feedback as being absolute and unequivocal not only assumes an omnipotence to which no one outside the Vatican can lay claim, but moves the relationship to one where the leader is saying, "The only way to get on around here is to *agree with me*." In an age of uncertainty, perfection is a somewhat overrated quality. To coach is to know that if you strip the employee of dignity you rob the organization of possibility.

In coaching *timing is everything*. For example, the best time to give feedback is as close to the critical incident being coached around as possible. However, it is sometimes more appropriate to give *negative* feedback immediately prior to the employee having an opportunity to put the new behavior into practice. Allowing a negative image to swirl around in the employee's head without the opportunity to correct it magnifies its potency and increases the probability that *the behavior we don't want* will be repeated.

Coaching is a discipline. The dictionary describes a discipline as a "training of the mind and character…a set of practical rules." Seven *practical* rules describe the rigor and character that a successful leader brings to the coaching conversation.

1. *The coach is the custodian of the organization's vision, values and leadership competencies.* This means the coach must have a deep insight into the organization's vision, values and overarching leadership competencies, and be personally committed to them. The coach must be forceful in challenging the employee who suggests a way forward that is misaligned with the organization's vision, values and leadership competencies and be open and candid about the leadership competencies which he/she (the coach) is focusing on. The coach is not expected to be perfect. The coach quickly becomes part of the problem if his/her comments and feedback are riddled with hypocrisy and apparent double standards.

2. *What the coach believes is more important than what the coach says.* More than ninety percent of what and how we communicate lies outside the specific content of the message. Intonations, nuance, body language, and breaking rapport all signal to the employee the real message. We are all highly attuned to pick up these signals, at both a conscious and subconscious level. The coach who says one thing (you can achieve this goal) but believes another (no way this is going to happen) is not only sowing the seeds of confusion but also destroying that most precious of commodities, trust. Simply put: what the coach believes is what the employee perceives.

3. *At the heart of what it means to coach is the capacity for emptiness.* Imagine two pieces of music, the first a piece by Sibelius, the second, classic Rolling Stones. Each is special…each is unique. On their own they have a vibrancy and quality that one cannot ignore. Play both at the same time, however, and the discordant jumble of noise is disturbing and ugly. Coaching means turning down the volume of one's own thoughts so that only the sound of the employee's music can be heard. To coach is to jettison the predetermined agenda, to silence the inner voice that calls attention to other priorities, to create the emotional space for new ideas to be heard, and to let go of past assumptions and beliefs that limit what is possible. To coach is to have the capacity to quiet the mind. To coach is to be totally present. To coach is to be in the moment. To coach is to learn how to, figuratively speaking, kick the mud off our shoes.

4. *A coaching conversation assumes that the answer lies with the employee.* For those who have spent a lifetime being rewarded for solving problems, this is by far the most difficult discipline to acquire. Once the problem has been tabled it is as if an irresistible force literally *makes* us want to come up with potential solutions. And when the employee does come up with a way forward and we "just know" we have a better way,

it takes an act of supreme willpower to hold those "better" ideas back. Coaching is *not* problem solving. A great coach presents his/her suggestions as a very last resort. There are two reasons for this: the first, ownership and commitment are synonymous; the second, it is assumed the employee has the answer simply because ninety percent of the time he/she actually does.

Dialogue built on the belief that the answer lies with the employee does not imply that the coach is a mute partner in the coaching conversation. When the employee suggests a future scenario that is not aligned with the emerging culture the coach

The role of the coach is to help the employee erect the "scaffolding" of self-discovery.

must challenge the employee's assumptions. When the employee says something that stirs the coach deeply, lack of emotional honesty erodes trust. And when the coach feels that self-disclosure, feedback, story, metaphor and/or conceptual insight would allow the employee to reach beyond him/herself, it would be an act of coaching negligence not to introduce those new points of reference.

Each of us has deep, empowering, inner resources that we ignore. The role of the coach is to help the employee erect the "scaffolding" of self-discovery. To coach is to guide the employee past his/her self-imposed barriers. To coach is to open up new possibilities. To coach is to enable the employee to move into new territory. To coach is to enrich the conversation the employee has with him/herself. To coach is to make the employee aware that the inner voice that whispers, "It's beyond me" is merely masking one that lies deeper within us, one that longs to shout, "Let's do it!"

Coaching is an act of support and not a mission of rescue. When the coach's "music" starts to dominate, when "telling" rather than "asking" becomes the underlying tone, little, if any, coaching is taking place. In coaching we are, in essence, coaching the employee to coach him/herself. It is a shift of focus that can only take place if the coach knows when and how to get out of the way.

5. ***To coach is to share the gift of presence…a deep awareness that makes listening a holistic experience.*** Most of us are poor listeners. Thirty percent listening efficiency is not at all unusual even amongst senior executives. Our listening skills are impaired by distractions…by the reality that we have a listening capacity that far exceeds the speed at which people speak…that we use this spare space to "script write" our response before the speaker has finished…that we make assumptions about the worth of the speaker even before he/she has spoken…and that we allow the clutter in our head to overwhelm the potential of the message. To coach is to listen. To coach is to listen for and not to listen to. To listen is not just a head and hand experience. We start to listen unconditionally when we open our heart and tap into that spiritual part of our makeup that is about caring. When we become judgmental, offer a caution, make suggestions,

or interrupt we are, in essence, saying, "I want to talk about me…not listen to you."

This magic of listening is described simply and beautifully in a *Tuesdays with Morrie: an old man, a young man, and life's greatest lesson* by Mitch Albom. "He did this better than anyone I'd ever known. Those who sat with him saw his eyes go moist when he spoke about something really horrible, or crinkle in delight when they told him a really bad joke. He was always ready to display the emotion so often missing from my baby boomer generation. We are great at small talk: 'What do you do?' 'Where do you live?' But really listening to someone – without trying to tell them something, pick them up, recruit them, or get some sort of status in return – how often do we get this any more? I believe many visitors in the last few months of Morrie's life were drawn not because of the attention they wanted to pay to him but because of the attention he paid to *them*. Despite his personal pain and decay, this little old man listened the way they always wanted someone to listen."[2] To coach is to listen the way *we* always wanted to be listened to!

> *Trust is to fly a kite and feel that no matter how hard the wind blows the string won't break.*

6. ***To coach is to ask artful questions…to probe without pushing, to challenge without forcing, to inquire without intruding.*** Asking questions is unquestionably the "art" of coaching. In normal, everyday conversation eighty percent of questions are statements in disguise. In the coaching conversation, if the spinning lathe represents the dialogue, questions become the tools that shape the outcome of the endeavor. As a result the coach selects his/her "tools" with care and uses each with sensitivity and a touch born out of experience. Two question formats are invaluable: inquiry and breakthrough. The first asks the employee, "Say more about that." "Go deeper." "Explore the alternatives." Silence in the hands of an experienced coach can be a masterful inquiry question. Breakthrough questions seek to challenge the employee's assumptions and beliefs; move the employee from today into tomorrow; shift the thinking from problem to opportunity; draw out what is missing; and/or test commitment. All meaningful learning starts with a question.

Great questions are a matter of timing and content. Timing is the coach's ability to recognize "the moment." Largely a combination of intuition and experience, knowing when to ask a question is as important as the question itself. The actual quality of the question owes much to the coach's teaching point of view[3]. The teaching point of view is the gift that the coach brings to the coaching conversation. It is often a straightforward proposition or belief, e.g. speed and simplicity. In my own case the head, the hand, the heart and the spirit – although not necessarily framed in that language – is the source from which many of my own coaching questions are drawn. A rich and meaningful teaching point of view builds shared mindsets. It creates continuity between coaching conversations. It brings common language to the coaching experience and it is a critical

---

[2] Pages 137 and 138

[3] Noel Tichy in his book, *The Leadership Engine,* used the term "teachable point of view."

ingredient in shaping team performance. To be a masterful coach is to have a teaching point of view.

7. *Coaching without trust is dance without music.* Like teamwork and culture, trust is a word that has great currency but one that often lacks shared meaning. Trust starts with the ability to build *rapport*. Trust is about *respect*. Trust is about *understanding* the other person's point of view. Trust is about *shared values*. Trust is the *capacity and drive* to deliver that which has been promised. Trust is the vessel that "breeds" enthusiasm. Trust is to fly a kite and feel that no matter how hard the wind blows the string won't break. Conversely, arrogance, in whatever form, is a dress rehearsal for a future devoid of trust. (See Chapter Nine.)

Building trust leads one to the realization that at some point coaching must encompass not just the individual, but also the team that surrounds him or her. Coaching that does not take the team into account is unlikely to result in either deep or lasting change.

The value of a coaching model?

The value of a coaching model goes without saying. A map that guides the uninitiated across new territory while at the same time allowing the expert to better reflect on his/her approach is a seductive notion. And here we should not forget the worth of such a model in coaching others in how to coach.

The difficulty is that any disciplined evaluation of coaching reveals that an experienced coach will have evolved his/her own particular style and approach. Even casual observation displays that the same coach, depending upon the opportunity, often starts (and sometimes ends) in a different place. The reality: every coaching conversation by way of direction and flow is, and should be, unique. The conclusion: the coaching discussion does not always follow a linear path, and a model that is built exclusively around that assumption runs the risk of being misleading.

Now for the good news. Although those well versed in the coaching art adopt what can best be described as a dynamic approach, underlying that outward appearance of chaos is invariably a common and very consistent pattern. What can be observed is less a model than it is a set of building blocks (template) that, regardless of the order they are brought into play, provide the framework (social architecture) for a successful coaching conversation.

Figure eight outlines that template. The successful coach treats each building block as one might the separate shapes in a jigsaw puzzle: each piece a distinct but essential part of the whole. Like the jigsaw it's the final picture and not the order in which the pieces are delivered that matters. Unlike a puzzle where there is only one solution, however, the coaching conversation is open-ended, the final picture limited only by the imagination and commitment of those involved. A typical coaching conversation might well proceed as follows:

Step one: *define the critical issue/opportunity.* The issue as first surfaced is often not the real issue. As a result, defining (uncovering) the issue is invariably a process of discovery, guided by the coach. It goes without saying, the issue is just as likely to be an opportunity as it is a barrier to performance. The critical issue could well be a shift the employee needs to make the organization's values live. It could focus on a competency that the employee displays excellence in, that he/she does not bring to the table often enough. The greatest leverage comes, however, when the coaching conversation is linked to *untapped potential in the business.*

Step two: *explore and agree what future performance success looks like.* The more specific the employee, guided by the coach, is in describing tomorrow's success the better. It is helpful if the employee creates/shares his/her own video of what tomorrow's success looks like and feels like. In that we cannot differentiate between imagery and the real thing, developing a future-oriented mental picture not only creatively explores what is

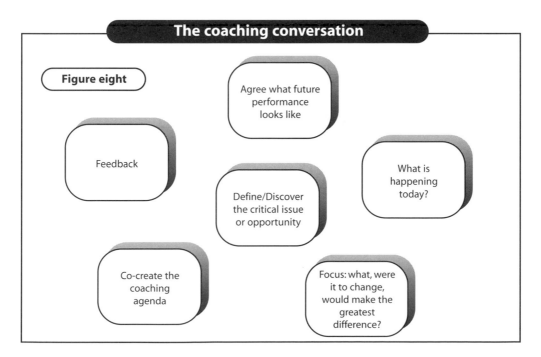

The coaching conversation

Figure eight

Agree what future performance looks like

Feedback

What is happening today?

Define/Discover the critical issue or opportunity

Co-create the coaching agenda

Focus: what, were it to change, would make the greatest difference?

possible, but also makes a desirable tomorrow more likely. This "video" has to be translated into (1) quantifiable *business* outcomes, and (2) the behaviors needed to deliver those outcomes.

Step three: build agreement about **what is happening** now. As with defining future success, the more specific the nature of the discussion the better. The key is to bridge how the employee behaves with *what's happening in the business*.

Step four: the coaching conversation should capture only one issue at a time. Focus is essential. Based on the gap between today's reality and tomorrow's success, the challenge is to agree on ___*the* issue that, were it to change, would make the greatest difference.__

Step five: describes the need to develop an action plan while at the same time pulling together the resources needed to act. An ideal action plan should be specific, time bounded, attainable, and aligned with the organization's vision and values. It is important that the coach and the employee *co-create the agenda* because the coach often has access to resources (e.g. opening up new opportunity, team support, training budget, expanding the employee's role) not unilaterally available to the employee. What is being sought is a deep understanding of the way forward, not a superficial sense of consensus. The agenda must embrace not just the behaviors involved *but how the business will be impacted* by the change agreed to. The agenda, once agreed, is a binding commitment.

Step six: a dimension of any development and/or performance conversation should be to agree when the coach and the employee will review the extent to which the employee has been successful in delivering on the commitment. The latter should include both the behaviors involved and how the business has been impacted by the changes that have taken place. Such planned *feedback* is, of course, complemented by appropriate "in-the-moment" conversations.

Like many coaching conversations, the steps outlined focus initially on **the critical issue**. As pointed out, the coaching conversation does not always take the obvious (linear) path. This can be seen in the coaching approach of Jan, an outstanding coach who leads a high performance sales team.

In the scenario being described, Jan gets together with one of her sales executives in a small coffee shop, following a meeting with a key account customer. Jan attended the meeting but deliberately played a low-key role. Her whole reason for being there was to work with the sales executive. These curbside conferences are where Jan does her best work. Because of the depth of the relationship and the respect between the two, Jan opens up the coaching conversation by giving *feedback*. The "I think" language is very apparent. Jan then draws out from the executive his ideal view of future success with this customer. The conversation moves to **what is happening today**, and the barriers that prevent this ideal situation from unfolding. Only now does the sales executive, prompted by artful questions, identify **the critical issue**. Having agreed on the critical issue (lack of a *winning* value proposition) the conversation moves on to capture **the one thing that were it to change would make the greatest difference**, in this case the business opportunities that would potentially unfold were the sales executive to bundle other attributes into the value proposition. Moving forward, **creating the coaching agenda** embraces setting out and agreeing on both the business outcome (potential sales with this customer) and the behavioral goals (how the executive will act differently). Creating the agenda also involves defining the skill development needed to allow the executive to move from being a "top gun" salesman to a key account executive. They agree to meet again in six weeks.

Jan's mastery as a coach allows her to orchestrate the coaching session to fit the opportunity. With the experienced sales executive she felt comfortable entering into the coaching conversation by giving *feedback*. With a new sales executive she would have been far less direct; she would likely have begun by asking him/her to identify the **issues** he/she faces. In coaching a colleague struggling with career issues she might well have entered into conversation by asking that colleague to describe his/her definition of *future success* (his/her vision). In coaching another member of the key account team the starting point could well have been **what is happening?**

Figure eight is especially valuable when the time available to coach is brief. In-the-moment coaching is the stock-in-trade of those who support line executives, e.g. human resource professionals. "Measure twice and cut once" is a good axiom when your role is to suggest "new plays." The coach is greatly helped, therefore, by mentally reviewing the coaching template and considering the question: Where can I make the greatest difference? It may be honest feedback respectfully presented, or an artful question about tomorrow's success. It could be to draw out the one change that would make the greatest difference. Then again, it might be to challenge how success is going to be measured. The most important thing to remember: in-the-moment coaching is a precision strike, not carpet-bombing.[4]

The greatest challenge in the coaching arena is not so much the act of coaching, but in coaching others in how to coach. Road-tested by hundreds of executives on both sides of the Atlantic, including a number of talented CEOs, the coaching template (*Figure eight*) has been found to be both pragmatic and simple to follow. Hopefully, the question, "My 360° feedback

Coaching is always a journey of shared discovery.

---

[4] Carpet-bombing refers to air attacks that treat an area (e.g. city) as a single military objective as opposed to clearly identifying military objectives and attacking them individually.

says I have to improve as a coach, can you help me?" should not be quite so difficult to answer in the future.

Finally, even in the performance coaching conversation the coaching model does not need to remain a hidden asset. Coaching is always a journey of shared discovery. Sharing the "map" (*Figure eight*) with the coachee not only enriches the spirit of collaboration but also introduces a process that supports the employee in his/her own coaching work.

Mastery

If one watches a world-class performer, whether on the stage or on the playing field, two qualities, in particular, make those with true mastery stand out. The first: mastery means always having just a little more time than the other performers. It is as if he/she is working to a different clock. The second: to have reached mastery is to be totally aware of *everything* that is going on. Intense focus is complemented by a holistic awareness of the space he/she is working in. This awareness embraces the other players and the audience, and involves a heightened sensitivity to the echoes reverberating around the container within which the action takes place.

A masterful coach displays the same qualities. For the performer this is learned behavior. It is no different for the coach. It starts with a total commitment to coaching as a way to lead. It is honed constantly by the many opportunities to coach that occur during the day, both in and outside of work. The next time a hotel receptionist is less than helpful, don't get mad, see it as an opportunity to coach!

The master coach is the ruler of his/her domain. The employee may be doing all the work, but the coach is constantly working the context. The tools that the coach brings to shaping the context are apparent in the quality of the questions, the rapport, pacing, timing, poise, nuance of language and, above all else, the use of silence. To a leader language is, of course, everything. Toxic words such as "try" (presumption of failure) and "but" (everything that goes before is manipulation; everything that follows is the truth) do not belong in the coaching arena.

Mastery can be seen in the skill that a coach brings to "contracting" for the coaching conversation. The alternative, a coaching ambush, turns the conversation into something reminiscent of a visit to the dentist. "The contract" should cover off the what (head), the how (hand), the why (heart), and who gains (spirit). Where the coach and the employee know each other well, it is helpful to suggest that the upcoming conversation will touch on an issue the employee is passionate about. This is not to imply that it is appropriate to "sugar coat" an upcoming, potentially tough, coaching session. To coach is to manage expectations. To coach is to start every coaching conversation by contracting around the outcome(s), e.g., "What do you want to come out of this conversation?"

Mastery is also apparent in the way the coach moves into the conversation. Although they can be awkward with a new employee, and a major hurdle to overcome with very senior executives, the first few minutes of the coaching conversation set the scene. Mastery can be seen in the question, "Tell me your story." In sharing his/her story the coachee is revealing much about him/herself. What the coachee is passionate about signals what is *really* important. What the coachee omits often turns out to be his/her Achilles' heel. How the coachee describes success and/or failure is a window into his/her propensity for risk. The coachee's ability with language is an early indicator of an ability (or otherwise) to lead transformational change. The "we" versus "I" language says much about teamwork. Facing adversary, stability, attributing blame, candor, openness, self-criticism all speak to character, resilience and commitment. Even a short story will give the skilled listener insight into the coachee's balance between head, hand, heart and spirit. Sharing his/her story is also very meaningful for the person being coached. In hearing his/her own story the coachee is posing breakthrough questions to him/herself, "What is important?" "Where have I made a difference?" And that most challenging of questions, "Who am I?"

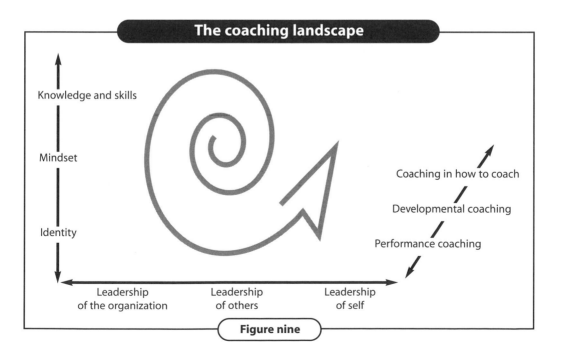

The coaching landscape

Figure nine

Mastery is found in the coach's understanding that not everyone changes at the same speed. One person needs to be pushed. Another needs time and space to process his/her thinking. To coach is to understand that several factors come into play in determining the speed at which the employee is likely to change. The following formula is one that the coach would do well keep in mind.

> *Speed of change* = The employee's past experience of change x the individual's capacity for change x emotional impact of the change – the unresolved change in the employee's life.

An airline pilot knows where he/she is in relation to everything else that is going on. The pilot knows when he/she is upside down, when he/she is facing the wrong direction and hopefully when he/she is in difficulty. This is part instinct, part training and part the pilot's ability to carry in his/her head – and correct in real-time – a three dimensional map of the space through which he/she is flying.

Mastery, similarly, lies in the coach's ability to know at all times where he/she is in the coaching conversation. (*See Figure nine.*)

In the coaching conversation the coach is always working concurrently on **three axes**. *The first*: the focus of the conversation, be it performance, development, or coaching in how to coach. *The second*: the nature of the challenge…leadership of the business, leadership of others and/or the leadership of self. *The third*: the level at which the change needs to take place…knowledge, skills, mindset and/or identity.

It is a brave, ambitious (and often naïve) coach who dives right into issues that fall under the banner of leadership of self. This is where the greatest change is likely to take place, and where much of the coaching conversation must be anchored. But moving too quickly, pushing without building trust, intruding without winning respect is likely to not only generate resentment but make the nature of the conversation around "self" shallow and lacking in authenticity.

Mindsets represent personalized filters through which we create our own sense of reality. All the dialogue in the world around new ways to act are of little value if the coachee believes that "bosship" and leading by telling is absolutely the only way to run a business. And the leader who preaches change but fails to recognize that his/her weekly meeting always takes place at 10.30, is always five minutes late, has an entirely predictable agenda and everyone always sits in the same chair, will not be helped by training alone. To coach is thus to be able to work at the level of mindset.

Eventually, if we dig down deep enough we come to identity. Identity describes a way to be. Identity is who we are. Identity is our personal path to mastery. The coach cannot change a person's identity. An individual may modify elements of their identity (e.g. we can become more extroverted as we get older) and a traumatic event may impact our identity in a dramatic way but, for the most part, we are who we are. This is important for the coach to understand because a good deal of time is spent within organizations trying to make people fit into a role for which they are totally ill-equipped. Oh, they may have the skills, and the diploma on the wall says that they are qualified, but underneath they do not have, as Thomas Wolfe put it, "The Right Stuff." The tragedy is that in an appropriate role that same employee might very well soar. (See Chapter Ten.)

Conclusion

Armies since the time of Alexander the Great have been dogged by a single misguided belief: the way forward is to train and equip themselves to ensure victory in yesterday's battles. Even late in World War I – the era of the machine gun – cavalry was still regarded by many of the generals as the way to break through the German lines. Constructed in the 1930s, the Maginot Line was built in northeastern France based on the assumption that if war came again it would be fought as in WWI, in fixed lines of fortified trenches. Intercontinental ballistic missiles have little relevance in a world where the enemy attacks with box knives and use the mail as its weapon delivery system.

Leaders seduced into thinking they can control much outside their own behavior are, likewise, destined to focus on battles that have already been fought. The reality: the policies and procedures written to establish control are totally worthless the instant someone changes the game. Early models of the horseless carriage had to have a man with a red flag walk in front of the vehicle. It was a rule that became redundant the moment it became apparent that the automobile could travel significantly faster than any man. Attempts to establish hard rules for something that cannot be anticipated (paradoxically) only make sense if seen as the product of an irrational mind.

To lead today is to unleash the hounds: dramatically simplify the role of the center, make strategy an operational issue, push decision-making as close to the customer as possible and burn the rule book. The first step is to hire and promote leaders who are ultra-comfortable with ambiguity and who, in addition, possess the character and courage to reinvent the business as needed. What takes the place of hierarchy and rules? Agility of thought and action are only possible where there is a passionate commitment to a common culture: vision, values, leadership competencies, measurement, shared language, end-to-end value flow… all supported by a highly innovative learning platform.

Somewhere in the mix is speed: testing people earlier, stripping down the business processes to their optimum delivery potential, speed of action in the marketplace and, of course, speed of learning.

Coaching lies nestled at the center of the new work for leaders. Freedom to act without support is a recipe for confusion and unnecessary conflict. Challenging the status quo without know-how plays into the hands of the cynics. Innovation without alignment guarantees value destruction. And learning without coaching is like watching a bullfight where someone forgot to invite the bull.

Any leader who wants to make it in the future and believes coaching is a nice to have, but non-essential, capability had better hope we don't run out of organizations where the rules, control, and "power in the hands of the few" still dominates. And yet, much as it is heralded, coaching is still a relatively low priority for many leaders, still something he/she would like to do better but not something that finds its way to the top of the "to do" list.

For those leaders who do not see coaching in their future the answer is clear...*fail now, save time later!* Fortunately, those who believe that coaching is the prerogative of the few need only to start to coach to realize that they are already hardwired for the task. And for those struggling to find the time to coach, an earlier comment is worth repeating, "How do successful leaders find the time to spend 60% of their time coaching?" Their answer, "I spend 60% of my time coaching because... I spend 60% of my time coaching." Go work that gene!

What to do differently on Monday

1. Outsourcing coaching sends a very strong message about what it means to be a leader. Ask anyone who offers his/her services as an external coach what his/her teaching point of view is. Push for organization-wide coaching protocols. Outsource performance coaching as a last resort.

2. The only way to become a masterful coach is to coach. Contract for a coaching conversation with one of the champions on your team. Think about the seven practical rules of coaching outlined in the Chapter. Evaluate yourself against each of the seven "rules." Draw up a development plan putting the element (out of the seven) that represents your greatest strength at the top of the list. Put where you need to make the greatest improvement at the bottom. Ask for feedback. Commit to work on all of the elements.

3. Review and understand the six steps in the coaching conversation diagram. Use this as the outline for your next coaching conversation. It may even be a good idea to share the six steps with the coachee.

4. Conduct the coaching session.

5. Take time out to reflect on the success of the coaching conversation. Define what you need to do differently. Ask for feedback. Grow as a coach by asking to be coached. Seek out a masterful coach to work with you.

Book Three

Leadership

of Self

Chapter eight

Leadership of self: three currents, one stream

Book Three
Leadership of Self

As it gently kisses the landscape, the first light of early dawn creates a subtle hue of blue, green and golden brown. Within minutes the sun will be a magnificent orange. Just as quickly it will transform itself again into a brilliant source of light that, for the nocturnal animals of the Bushveld will signal not the beginning, but the end of another day.

At first, the animal's shape is difficult to make out. What is apparent is the gentle breeze, nature's ever-constant messenger, an early morning companion that carries, to those watching, the earthy smell of the Savannah. The rhino stands motionless, moving his enormous head only to check for danger. For one brief moment of perfection, the watchers and nature stand in harmony.

It is this vast expanse of beauty that the rhino calls home. And, as he moves forward threateningly, the watchers are suddenly reunited with a primeval fear as old as man himself. Were he to charge, two tons of muscle, bone, and raw power would be cannoning towards the watchers at a speed comparable to that of an Arabian stallion.

The rhino being watched is referred to by a number only: Number 15. He is a dominant male. He marks his territory with piles of dung, for he is truly territorial. Other males that enter his territory must expect to fight. Teamwork, a sense of togetherness, working in harmony, count for less than naught to Number 15. His is a world where control and dominance rule.

He snorts loudly, and his discomfort is apparent. The watchers know enough not to move. Rhinos are very short sighted; although the watchers are less than forty feet away, Number 15 can't see them. He doesn't charge. The moment passes and the watchers become conscious of the sound of something other than the weight of silence: the cry of a bird, the buzz of an insect, the chatter of a baboon. And, as the watchers raise their eyes towards the horizon, they see other animals: a gemsbok, several buffalo and, only a little further away, a small herd of zebra.

The watchers are caught up in the age-old rhythm of Africa. It is a beat that lies at the very center of our being. It is a haunting cadence that for thousands of generations dominated man's existence. It is a way to be and way to feel that is the very wellspring of who we are.

Number 15 is a perfect example of nature's complex and, at times, dramatic evolutionary plan. He is also sadly symbolic of an era that is past. A time before fences and guns. A time before poaching. A time before rhino horn was believed by many in the Orient to carry with it the powers of virility. A time before pollution. A time before man's immoral behavior to his animal kith and kin.

Number 15 is a powerful and magnificent beast. He is not, however, the master of his own destiny. He survives only through the generosity, recently discovered morality and, at times, morbid curiosity of his Homo Sapiens second cousins. It is all the sadder because Number 15's lumbering gait, angry snort, and blunt movement across the veldt has, for millions of years, been a lead musician in Africa's drumbeat of survival.

The rhino is a visual story of Africa, a transcending message that captures the nature and challenge facing those in man's historical homeland. Underpinning the imagery, deep in the consciousness of the watchers, channeling raw emotion into awareness, much as the great rivers of Africa are transported along underlying bedrock, is the raw music of Africa, an incessant rhythm that sings out, "To survive is to change."

It matters not that the watchers are a group of executives whose work is to draw nature's precious minerals from up to a mile below Africa's parched earth – for in a real sense they are each of us. Where goes Africa, so walks the rest of mankind. It has always been thus. None of us lives in a hermetically sealed cave. The New York stockbroker in some small indelible way shares the stark canvas of Stone Age life in the Kalahari. We all play our part to perpetuate a surreal world where AIDS, famine, and intertribal wars are juxtaposed with a desire for yet more sophisticated weapons of destruction. The irreplaceable loss of the rainforest, the unconscionable destruction of ocean life, youth violence and the sharp decline in male sperm count, all suggest that the path the rhino so perilously treads today is one that we also walk.

The leadership each of us encounters with man's greatest struggle comes to us as a distant and faint echo of the one that screams to be heard in the encounter with Number 15. We are part of that struggle nevertheless. To grow is to recognize that all living creatures are inexorably bound. Impact one part of the system and the turbulence created changes the whole. To survive is to evolve. To stay as we are is to pass the responsibility for the quality of our own life and that of our children's lives to those who would have us believe that within short-term material gain lies the elixir of life.

Our role has been cast and our performance unfolds on a smaller stage than that portrayed by the sweeping majesty of the African plains. Our brush with destiny lies with our local community, our family and ourselves. This is our habitat. The contribution we make to society, the way we bring up our children, the example we set, determines what is important long after we leave this place. It is *within*, however, that the journey begins. To positively impact the lives of others, to make a contribution beyond our immediate egocentric needs, to leave a lasting heritage, to lead, we must first know ourselves.

To discover ourselves is perhaps life's greatest challenge. What follows is, of necessity, incomplete. The path to self-knowledge unfolds over a lifetime. It is a journey that, in the words of Joseph Campbell, "moves you into your own loneliness." It is an epic adventure that demands awareness, balance, courage and discipline. It is a quest for a rich and vibrant life. It is a voyage of self-discovery that follows three streams of consciousness.

1. We become what we dream

If we can learn anything from Number 15 it is that in a world marked by social and economic turbulence, each of us, either as individuals or as a part of a wider community, has to define our own path of evolution – we must create our own tomorrow. Paradoxically, it is a philosophy of action likely to be enacted only where those in question recognize that within tomorrow's sweeping patterns of change lies today's opportunity.

Dreamers know that only those who can see what isn't there can deliver what isn't possible.

To dream is to dare. To dream is to reach beyond the mundane and imagine the barely possible. To dream is to celebrate one's uniqueness. To dream is to cast aside the shackles of ordinariness and inhabit a world where we are the most and the best we can be. No one presents this better than Antoine-Marie-Roger de Saint-Exupéry (see also Chapter Three) who wrote: "A rock pile ceases to be a rock pile the moment a single man contemplates it, bearing within him the image of a cathedral."[1]

To dream is to rehearse in the theatre of the mind, tomorrow's success. The most compelling dreams are those that live with full force in the imagination. The dreams that chart a new

[1] *Flight to Arras.*

way to be are those that weave imagery, touch, and smell into a rich and seamless experience. Not to dream is to pass the baton to those who do.

To dream is touch our uniqueness. To dream is to become conscious that we are far more than that described in the script that others have written for us. To dream is to connect with the inner voice that narrates our personal story. To dream is to surface and set in motion the opportunity to live and fulfill that story.

That inner voice, filtered by our personality, directs our intentions. Our intentions, in turn, provide the script for conscious behavior. Our stories are the essence of who we are, but along the way they pick up sub-plots that speak of failure. Before we can live our dream we must, therefore, first audition ourselves for the new role that the dream implies. Are we worthy? Are we committed? Do we have the discipline? In answering affirmatively we give ourselves permission to listen to, debate, seek evidence for, dialogue with, argue against, and, when demanded, contradict that which we tell ourselves limits what we are capable of being. Only then do we start to develop wisdom drawn out of an understanding that when we avoid rather than confront our problems, we limit our growth. And only then are we likely to develop the inner resources needed to face and cast aside that which holds us back.

A dream is an act of self-fulfillment wrapped in a paradox. Dreamers know that only those who can see what isn't there can deliver what isn't possible. That does not mean that the dreams that move us forward are the same as speculation, wishful thinking or fantasy. Dreams are fueled by imagination but are anchored in reality. To dream is to create a tomorrow that folds the art of the possible around a tough-minded pragmatism – leaders have deadlines.[2]

Dreams that empower are rooted in intent. The companion of intent is courage. Courage is to embrace risk. Courage is standing alone. Courage is saying no. Courage is not letting go of the dream. Here one is reminded of the words of Henry David Thoreau: "If one advances confidently in the direction of his dreams, and endeavors to live the life he has imagined, he will meet with a success unexpected in the common hours."

If anyone had a right to give up on the dream it was the legendary baseball player, Jackie Robinson. The first black player in the National League when he signed for the Brooklyn Dodgers in 1947, his first season in the majors would have been a trial for any man.

Through dreams we become our own hero.

For someone as proud as Robinson, who had dragged himself from poverty to become a college graduate and an army officer, it was a living hell. Even the owners had voted 15-1 against bringing him into the majors. Deeply resented by some of his southern

---

[2]   In his book *On Becoming A Leader,* Warren Bennis suggests, "Leaders are dreamers with a deadline."

team members, he couldn't board in many of the hotels where his teammates stayed, or even eat in the same restaurants. Being spat at, vocally abused, spiked, and deliberately tagged on the head was commonplace. In that first year he was hit by more balls than any other player in the league. Robinson's response: to turn anger into excellence, fear into determination and mistrust into performance. He was voted Rookie of the Year. Two years later he was the National League's most valuable player. He was instrumental in getting the Dodgers into six World Series, played on six All-Star teams, and in 1972 was voted into Baseball's Hall of Fame.

Throughout history we have been inspired by the hero.[3] The darker the night, the more welcome the illumination from a single candle. Overawed by the challenge, reluctant at first, but magnificent when the battle is enjoined, the hero succeeds only if he or she is first prepared to tear away the burden of personal doubt. Through dreams we become our own hero.

A dream that remains hidden cannot be realized. To dream alone is to revel in loneliness. Sharing our dream with others is to invite them into a sacred space. Helping others surface their dreams is an act of generosity drawn out of a serving spirit. Dreams that lie behind a veil, dreams that are not given wing, like an eagle tethered to its perch, lead to assumptions that to soar is the prerogative of others. To lead is to help others take flight.

A dream that enriches one's life is born of the spirit. A dream that evokes passion dwells in the heart. A dream that empowers engages the hand. A dream that sustains appeals to the head. Sharing our dream is a richer and deeper vehicle of self-expression than that portrayed through the "one size fits all" vision statement. We share our dream not through a framed statement from the corporate office, but through story. In story we share not only what we desire, but who we are.

2. *To know oneself, one must be authentic*

The dictionary defines authenticity as "truth." It is impossible to know who we are unless our approach to others is anchored in authenticity.

To be authentic is to resolve moral and ethical dilemmas, not by analyzing what is expedient, but by asking the question, "Is the course of action I am about to take aligned with what I believe in?" Leadership drawn out of authenticity naturally leads to consistency of purpose and behavior. Lack of authenticity destroys the spirit.

To be authentic is to take pride in accomplishment, but to realize that our journey is made possible by the generosity of others. Authentic leaders respond to this debt by displaying

---

[3] For hero read also heroine.

loyalty to those who helped him or her along the way, and by sharing their talent with others. To share is to learn.

To be authentic is to live with awareness of, and consideration for, the broader issues that make up the leadership challenge. Authenticity lies in a basic respect for the lifestyle of others. Authenticity lies in the response to poisoned waterways, child-slavery in the third world and the homeless on our city streets. Leadership that lacks a sense of "community" destroys the spirit. To be authentic is to care. Caring, like enthusiasm, is infectious.

To be authentic is to listen – to listen not for what is said but what is meant. Authentic leaders listen because they are driven to be "interested," not by a desire to appear "interesting." Authentic leaders know what will work because they have the capacity to see the world as others see it. To be authentic is to listen and only then to act.

To be authentic is to be vulnerable. To be authentic is to find the courage to strip away the mask that we use to protect ourselves from that part of ourselves we keep hidden. To be authentic is to know our own secrets. To be authentic is to stand emotionally naked and ask "Who am I?" To be authentic is to listen to the answer. To be authentic is to ask not why, but why not? In sharing our vulnerability with others we give them permission to tear away their own mask.

To be authentic is to strive for honesty in the dialogue we have with ourselves. Inner dialogue that is rooted in truth transforms life's unforeseen events into learning experiences. Self-talk anchored in self-delusion provides little shelter when storm clouds break. When we have lost touch with who we are, criticism, a perceived slight, even a mild rebuke gives rise to a response that is disconnected from reality.

To be authentic is to rid ourselves of the outdated maps that others have drawn for us.

To be authentic is to rid ourselves of the outdated maps that others have drawn for us. To be authentic is to chart our own course. To be authentic is to accept both criticism and praise with openness. It is within this striving for authenticity that the difference between a friend and an acquaintance becomes apparent, that the difference between a commitment and a goal is surfaced, and the difference between want and need is truly understood. To be authentic is to rid ourselves of the burden of constantly striving for that which others tell us we must have.

To be authentic is to constantly seek models, concepts and examples that question the status quo. Authenticity demands not just an openness to see the world anew, but a passion for feedback. Authentic leaders see feedback as the lifeblood of self-development and personal growth. They perceive well-designed 360° instruments and response from the customer as being integral to the leadership process. Authentic leaders ask to be coached, and seek out the most able person available. Authentic leaders receive negative feedback with openness, and positive feedback with humility. When advice and counsel is given, they take time to reflect on the implications.

To be authentic is to purge our lives of toxic personalities and others that demand that we live in a way that does not nurture our spirit. This does not mean avoiding conflict, the absence of risk, or a reluctance to live and learn at the edge. It is merely recognition that we cannot live and thrive if we are forced to live out our lives as if we exist in a series of isolated domains. What pollutes one part of our being impacts our whole being. When our actions are disconnected from who we are we take something away from that which we are capable of in *everything* we do. Attempts to maintain respect for those who don't deserve that respect eventually destroys our own self-respect. When we cheat ourselves we cheat those who care for us.

3. *Fear makes us strong*

Imagine the scene. This is the organization's annual executive meeting. The large auditorium is full. Your peers sit in the hope that you, the afternoon speaker will be as engaging and humorous as the individual who spoke before lunch. And she was humorous. Off-stage you pace nervously. You didn't really want to do this but you didn't know how to say no. The executive introducing you is so good it's embarrassing. Finally, his introduction comes to an end. You are on. There is respectful applause. You move slowly to center stage. This is the moment of truth. Success can propel you forward. A mid-winter safari to admire the fauna of northern Manitoba was the reward for the last one who failed.

For many, this is a terrifying moment. Fear takes over. Fear dominates. Fear drives out weeks of practice and replaces it with a deep sense of impending doom.

The answer is not to work to rid ourselves of fear. Fear is hardwired into our nervous system. Fear, and its partner adrenaline, is what saved us when we first stood erect. Fear breeds anticipation. Fear makes us strong. We can no more rid ourselves of fear than we can shed our skin.

Flight from fear is not the strategy of the professional actor. For him or her, fear is a welcome friend, to be embraced, used, breathed in as if it were sea air on an ocean cruise. For the actor, fear sharpens the senses. It heightens the ability to focus. Fear nourishes. Fear is the very essence of awareness. Fear hones the professional performer's edge. Without fear there can be no progress. Without fear there is no hero.

A life full lived is not about avoiding stress. To hide, to avoid challenge, to be anchored firmly in the center of our comfort zone is to deny growth. The existentialist philosopher Kierkegaard wrote, "There is an adventure that every human being must go through – to learn to be anxious in order that he may not perish. Whoever has learned to be anxious in the right way has learned the ultimate…the more profound he is in anxiety, the greater is the man."

> *The most difficult barriers to overcome are the ones we erect ourselves.*

The Chinese character for "crisis" is made up of two elements – one means danger and the other emphasizes opportunity. Fear is also comprised of two competing forces. The energy lies not in either one but in the tension that is produced as each calls out for attention. The echo of one says that moving forward means failure and change means losing that which we have. The alternative voice says avoiding risk leads to stagnation, taking a new path renews possibility, and living life at the edge lets you be who you are capable of being. The voice we condition ourselves to pay heed to determines the path we take.

It takes more than a sense of dissatisfaction for those bathed by its heat to leave the comfort of the campfire. Heading out into the desert commits us to the new order of things, forces us to understand why the journey is necessary and to know who gains. The responsibility that we take with us is but one burden. The heaviest load we must carry is that which exists in our consciousness. The most difficult barriers to overcome are the ones we erect ourselves.

Fear of success dwells in the hidden recesses of our mind. Fear of success is, in reality, a fear of self. It is a deep-rooted vulnerability that, in some measure, resides within each of us. For those locked into a self-image that is discordant with the new reality the emotional load can be overwhelming. Success can be liberating or it can be a jail cell. When the images we carry of ourselves and our assumptions come under attack, when we must be that which is in some ways alien to our upbringing, we are on a collision course with our very sense of identity. Moving forward lies in answering the question, "What do I need to let go of?" In seeking the answer we are marshalling the inner resources needed to overcome that which holds us back.

Fear is, in part, a matter of context. The Bushman who takes famine, drought and pestilence in his stride would find the "simple" act of crossing Wall Street during rush hour a terrifying experience. Then why are we surprised when an employee whose total work experience has been defined by a need to "follow the rules" and who is now asked to make decisions, is no less bewildered?

The classic organization model that dominated the past century was built on and used fear as the primary means to exercise control. The time clock, the rulebook, the policy manual, the discipline procedure, were all built on the assumption that "the worker" was not to be trusted. We seek to control those we need but do not trust. And as Machiavelli preached and every dictatorship has understood since, fear is the easiest and most certain way to exercise control.

The workers' response: supervisory boards, intense and often blind loyalty to an outdated trade union philosophy, distrust of management, censure of those who break ranks, a continued sense of entitlement, and a lack of willingness to share ideas. This is the world of Number 15: controlling, suspicious, powerful, magnificent even – but destined for extinction.

Three currents, one stream

Leadership of self describes three streams of consciousness: (1) the need for a dream, (2) the power of authenticity, and (3) the destructive forces unleashed by fear. Each is presented as a separate domain to facilitate understanding. In reality one is woven into the other, each integral to a larger sense of well-being. They are different currents and eddies that flow in the same stream.

Leaders who lack a dream have little cause to go to the edge. What they ignore is that a life of "comfort" strips away self-esteem and destroys initiative. Ambition devoid of a dream entails a life of game-playing, manipulation, and a dependency on perceived status as a means to maintain the illusion of success.

Lack of openness and authenticity follow a similar course. At a deep, instinctive, gut level, we know when we are not operating out of truth. When we live in the shadows we resist the unknown.

Fear is no less limiting. Fear that overwhelms leads to paralysis when action is needed. Fear that strangles courage attributes blame, when self-disclosure is the key to learning and growth. Fear that draws out the "why" rather than "why not" celebrates and perpetuates yesterday's ideas. Fear that prompts caution destroys the passion as surely and quickly as water douses the campfire.

One of the modern myths is that humans have an innate resistance to change. If that were the case we would still be striking rocks together to create fire. We would be carrying sharpened sticks as a means to secure lunch. A more current example lies with the avalanche of self-help books that fill bookstore shelves. Our drive to be ***the best we can be*** is compelling. It is the very essence of who we are. Our accompanying drive to change is no less emphatic. What is lacking is the courage to dream, the character needed to lead through authenticity, and the commitment demanded if the fear that holds us back is to be transformed into a force that will propel us forward. What is missing from the equation is self-leadership. To become more of who we are, we have to know who we are not.

Leadership, as taught in our red brick institutions, has long been dominated by the **head** and the **hand**. Conspicuous by its absence has been the leader's need to engage the **heart** and enrich the **spirit**. Short-term success – as measured by financial criteria – has led us to believe that head and hand leadership is sustainable. The fact that study after study shows that lack of leadership is an ill that has reached epic proportions suggests otherwise. Those who have power, but who cannot take others with them, do not lead. Those who seek to change others, but who do not themselves have the capacity to change, cannot succeed. Those who present a vision, but who themselves are not wedded to that dream, cannot enlist followership. The genesis of leadership lies not with the head and hand, but with the heart and spirit. It does not matter that there is a strategy to dominate the market place if the leader in question cannot incite passion. It counts for nothing that the business is rooted in superb organization design if the man or woman at the helm is not personally in touch with the leader within.

Ultimately, leadership is about balance. The need for personal goals (head) goes without saying. The demand for conscious skill development (hand) is apparent to all. Balance completes the weave. Leadership that dwells in the heart is taking pride in the growth of others. The heart is about love; it speaks to family and personal growth. The spirit describes our passion for life; it speaks to health and wellness. It is about what we eat, how we exercise and the need to set time aside for reflection. Spirit is about the meaning we draw from the things we do and about what we give back. Spirit is about leaving a legacy. Without balance we are incomplete as leaders. Without balance we give to others only part of what we have. Without balance we travel without integrity and arrive without companionship. Without balance, even acknowledged success inevitably evokes the question, "Was the journey worthwhile?"

The lineage of the modern rhino can be traced to China and a time long before man stood erect. Number 15 is a white rhino, one of only five species of rhino that still survive; five out of over 200 that have proudly walked the earth – including one colossus that was the largest land-based mammal and another that grew only to the size of a greyhound.

The rhino is, without doubt, an evolutionary masterpiece. It has survived volcanic upheaval, flood, and ice age. The current generation of human ape, however, will tragically be the last of their kind to see this noble beast in the wild.

The Irish elk similarly moved into extinction, not because it failed to evolve, but because its story of change left it misaligned with a rapidly changing environment. Caught in trees and bogged down by the weight of its ever-larger antlers it became, literally, a victim of its own evolutionary success. It is a lesson from the court of the Red Queen. It is a lesson that none of us should ignore.

What to do differently on Monday

1. Write down what you would do with your life if you had a one-year sabbatical with pay. Do it anyway!

2. Think of the toxic personalities in your life. Avoid those who always see the glass as "half empty." Part company with those who deal with a new idea by first telling you what they "know" to be wrong with it. Purge from your life those who hide their own insecurity behind a mask of cynicism. Such people suck the life out of your dreams, distort your need to be authentic, and gain satisfaction by amplifying the inner voice – the one that dominates their own lives – that says, "I am not worthy."

3. Go for a walk. Think about what it is that you fear most. Think through what would really happen if what you fear came to be. Know that you would survive. Know that you would deal with it. Know that it would make you stronger.

4. Think of those times when you succeeded against all the odds. Think about a time when you did what others didn't believe you could do. Set a new goal that will shock the naysayers even more.

5. Get up early and watch the sunrise. Be reminded that we have a sacred duty to protect and pass on that which we have inherited.

Chapter nine

It's all about trust

Book Three
Leadership of Self

Nicolas Evans' best selling book *The Horse Whisperer* describes a symbiotic relationship between a girl and her horse. It captures the guilt that a young woman feels for an animal injured so badly the local veterinarian begs the family to put it down. It speaks to a mother's love so deep she drives halfway across a continent pulling a horsebox with a half-crazed thoroughbred for companionship, to meet a cowboy she doesn't know.

Shattered dreams are transformed into hope by a simple man who understands that the first act in the drama of change lies in knowing ourselves. A journey of self-discovery is made possible by gentleness born of strength.

Montana's big sky is a magnificent setting. The pace and rhythm are engaging, the voice between the lines compelling. *The Horse Whisperer* displays all of these but it is more...much more. It is loved – and it is loved because it touches something deeper, something that each of us yearns for, a need so firmly rooted in our psyche that without it none of us is complete. It's all about trust!

Trust of self

Gandhi said, "Among the most essential qualities of the human spirit are to trust oneself and to build trust with others." You cannot be trusted if you do not trust, and you cannot trust others unless you first trust yourself. Although often portrayed as such, trust is far more than a set of skills to be applied. Trust is even more than a personal discipline. Trust, winning trust, and trusting are ways to live one's life that start, as they must, with knowing ourselves.

In Grade 3 she was diagnosed with dyslexia. As a teen, when she came down with a kidney infection, she was so poor that she was turned away from hospital after hospital. To pursue a music career both she and her mother moved into a van near the beach. To survive she wore castoff clothes and washed her hair in public washrooms. Her first album sold 500 copies. Undeterred, she played bars and hole-in-the-wall clubs. Disc jockeys refused to play her music and producers said she would never make it. At the ripe old age of twenty-two she sold 500,000 copies of her CD *Pieces of You*. Her second CD, *Spirit*, released a year later, sold three million copies. Her name is Jewel (Kilchner). She has a beautiful voice and stunning looks, but that's not what made her a success. Her secret: she didn't for a moment give up on herself.

Trust of self is what we tap into when the speed of the game means that we have to make rapid-fire, intuitive decisions. Trust of self is the cornerstone of collaboration, the wellspring of learning. Trust of self is the stretch in broadband leadership. Trust of self is the truth in storytelling and the reality check in talent acquisition. Without trust in self, coaching becomes just one more conversation. If you don't trust yourself you cannot know yourself. And knowledge of self is the gateway to mastery.

Trust of self is reflected in our values. None of us can build lasting commitment to that which has no meaning. Our values express what we believe in. Our values allow us to make the difficult choices. Values are the portal to self-awareness. Values are the wellspring of true character.

Our values also shape how others see us. To be trusted people need to know what those values are. To be trusted we must make sure our values are not blurred by a need to be right, look good, or fit in. To be trusted we must be the same person on Wednesday that we are on Monday and Tuesday.

We cannot give what we do not have. And what we give out is what we receive. If we are curious, new doors will open. If we are hopeful, new possibilities will unfold. If we are full of charity, what we will receive is joy. If we let the bigotry of others limit our possibilities we are handicapping ourselves. If we are always complaining, what we will hear are grievances. If we are full of anger, what we will get back in return is bitterness. If we lack generosity of spirit, we should not be surprised if others seem to lack empathy. If we don't support others, they will have no reason to support us. **If we don't trust... we will not receive trust!**

Let me share a personal story. While I was teaching on the executive MBA at the Helsinki University of Technology, a very talented young man drew attention to an issue with which he was struggling. His question followed a discussion around trust and the qualities of leadership demanded to deliver organizational change. His dilemma: his immediate boss was committed to bringing about change but possessed few of the qualities being described in the class. He added that it was clear from his perspective that if his boss were to continue along the current path, the full change agenda would not be realized. His question: could he afford to speak up? As he described it, his boss did not take criticism well and there was a strong possibility that the degree of honesty he deemed necessary would damage his immediate career prospects. Was going along, to get along, not the smart option? In the discussion that followed we concluded that he had a clear choice. He could sit back safely and hope that things worked out, or he could act! It was a decision fundamental to who he was and who he aspired to be. It was a decision that spoke to how much he trusted himself. Ultimately, solving his dilemma rested on one critical question: Am I a leader? A **manager** might go along, but a **leader** has no choice but to confront the issues. To do anything other than trust in himself was to give up any pretence that he was, or could become, the leader he wanted to be. Leaders ultimately must lead…even if the outcome is personally painful. It was William Jennings Bryant who said that, "Destiny is not a matter of chance, it is a matter of *choice*; it is not a thing to be waited for, it is a thing to be achieved."

A cult movie of the 60s, *The Ugly American* was a story set in a country that to all intents and purposes – although not by name – was Vietnam. At a press conference, when asked how to fight the ongoing war against communist aggression, the new ambassador, played by Marlon Brando, replies, "I'm saying we can't hope to win the Cold War unless we remember what we are for, as well as what we're against. I've learned…that I can't preach the American heritage and expect to be believed if I act out of impatience or sacrifice my principles to expediency. I've learned that the only time we're hated is when we stop trying to be what we started out to be 200 years ago."[1] Scriptwriter Stewart Stern's words offer a haunting reminder that in the act of reaching for the baton of leadership it's not just we as individuals, but nations that must first seek and then discover trust in self.

The building blocks of trust

How do you build trust? Trust is a gossamer thread: difficult to spin and oh, so easy to break. Somewhere in the middle of what it takes to develop trust there lies a "promise." The promise is often specific. In marriage it is set out as vows. A contract is a legal promise with consideration. Part of the promise is always implied; if I buy something that fails I expect you not just to fix it **but to give a damn**. Asking employees to complete a survey is a request containing an implied promise that the problems highlighted will actually get fixed… and not next year. Leaders, of course, don't wait that long! Often the promise is exclusively that which is implied (covert): I will help you but I expect that if I get into

---

[1] Universal Pictures (1963). Source: Globe and Mail newspaper, November 6, 2001

difficulty there will be reciprocity. Fulfilling the promise (all of it!) builds trust. Breaking the promise, not delivering part of it, failure to understand the implied element, lack of will to deliver, and the sound of trust being broken is, to those with an attuned ear, the organizational equivalent of hearing crystal crash against a marble floor.

When people think of the issues that create or destroy trust they are drawn to the big events, the times when delivery was spectacular or when the cost of failure was high. We are excited by the home runs, but it's consistently hitting singles that makes champions. Trust is no different. The chemistry of trust, a culture where people support each other, an environment where freedom to act flourishes, is ultimately the delivery of hundreds of implied promises. It is fulfilling these agreements of mutual self-interest and the trust that results that make any and every organization actually work. Structure is no more than organizational plumbing. For things to flow, someone has to actually turn the water on. Calling the customer back, being available at the time agreed, even answering the phone promptly can, in isolation, appear as insignificant actions. Nothing could be further from the truth. Collectively they are the glue that keeps all the other pieces together. Not unlike a focus on the small acts of crime in zero tolerance policing, building trust is sweating the small stuff. The greatest destroyer of trust isn't the broken contract, it's the lame excuse that starts with, "I'm sorry, I forgot."

Structure is no more than organizational plumbing. For things to flow, someone has to actually turn the water on.

The promise, grand or subtle, has four faces. All four are essential. Exclude one and the others count for naught.

There is trust of the **head**…communicating the vision, knowing the way forward, defining the outcome, having a strategy or plan that has been carefully thought through. Only an optimistic kid with a new compass wants to follow a leader who doesn't know – or can't communicate – where he/she is headed.

There is trust of the **hand**…the skills to build rapport, to communicate, to engage others. Rapport speaks to empathy. To communicate, to really communicate, means to see the world from the other person's point of view. Excellent listeners are at a distinct advantage when it comes to building trust.

Trust rests most easily with those who believe that when we come together the total is potentially greater than the sum of the parts. Life's Lone Rangers, the mavericks, and those who like to go it alone, run the risk, if they don't develop the discipline needed to keep others informed, of offsetting the value they create with the trust they erode. Keeping people informed is always part of the promise.

Time management plays a role in trust. Being late chips away at trust. Being ill-prepared does little to build trust. Not taking the time to coach eats away at the pillars of trust. And like a deathwatch beetle chomping its way happily through the legs of grandma's old table, the leader with a compelling need to micromanage is undermining the very foundation of what it means to build trust.

Complexity erodes trust. It's tough to be committed to something that is difficult to understand. Leaders who chase too many projects soon discover that the sighs of frustration and shouts of confusion drown out the language of trust. Focus engenders trust. Paradoxically, "Keep it simple" is not a simple thing to do. Simple, as pointed out in Chapter Six, should not be confused with "simplistic." And although it is often true that less is more, keeping it simple cannot be limited to merely stripping away the unnecessary. The simple message is the one that uses the words spoken by the audience. The simple approach rejects technical language in favor of story, imagery and metaphor to explain the way ahead. The simple message is one punctuated by "in the moment" feedback and supported by a philosophy of "catching them doing it right."

There is trust that emanates from the ***heart***…a true commitment for that being proposed. Trust comes from serving and not merely from service. Service is what we provide when things go wrong. It's part of the overt and specific promise. To serve is to care. It may not be written down but it always part of the promise. To serve is to respond. It is also to *care how people feel about the response*. To build lasting trust is to understand and act on the difference between serving and service.

The people we trust most are those who help us grow. High performers, in particular, are drawn to leaders who have an insatiable appetite to learn. Learning speaks to a natural curiosity, an openness to be coached and playfulness when exploring new ideas. At the same time, we are rightfully distrustful of the leader who speaks of the latest management "fad" but who lacks the personal discipline needed to discover what works and what doesn't.

There is trust of the ***spirit***…an underlying belief that the outcome of the venture being proposed enhances value for all those involved. Trust that is drawn out of the spirit cannot ignore the wider community. In countries where corruption is institutionalized, relationships develop that have the appearance of trust. The dilemma: all too often the assumed "trust" is short-lived. Rarely do such relationships outlive the opportunity for one of the parties to exploit a weakness in the other. This is one of reasons why, in such cultures, family is strongly integrated into business. In somewhat the same way that flying buttresses support early medieval churches, trust that lasts, trust that survives, is strongly aided if reinforced by societal standards that emphasize integrity as being central to the way business is conducted.

What happens in the wider community has a deep and lasting impact on business culture. Not too long ago families went out for the evening without locking their front door. Twenty years ago parents allowed their children to walk to school on their own. The breakdown in airline security is but one additional step in the gradual erosion of trust within society. "Progress" comes at a price. To ignore the impact of *life* on *work* is to significantly discount what it means to be a true leader. The reality: the need to rebuild trust within organizations is greater today then ever.

Trust that resides in the spirit is anchored in truth. Trust and truth come from the same Anglo-Saxon root *treowe*, meaning faith or truth. Leaders who operate from truth build trust. Leaders who avoid the truth, slant the truth, who use selective parts of the truth, and/or who withhold the truth for their own gain cannot, and do not, build trust.

Emotional honesty is an important characteristic of trust. We trust those who admit to being less than perfect. We are drawn to those who, when things go wrong, share how they feel. We respect the rider who falls then gets back in the saddle more readily than we do the one who claims to be perfect. Humility builds trust. Admitting when you're wrong builds trust. Saying, "I don't know" builds trust. Even asking for help builds trust.

Over the past decade much has been made of strategic alliances. Outsourcing, similarly, has become a way of life. The sad reality is that very few of these connections deliver that which is promised. The reason: few are based on trust. The plan looks good, the cost savings are difficult to dispute. The parties involved have been well trained in the art of negotiation. The problem: the "deal" is exclusively head and hand. What is missing: a deep and lasting commitment to the partnership (heart). What has been ignored is that if conditions change, a way needs to be found for *all* of those involved to share the pain or distribute the gain (spirit).

Trust is rooted in consistency

At the risk of disagreeing with Gandhi, it is more appropriate to talk of *re*building than building trust. On the Galapagos Islands the animals have no fear of man. A child trusts adults simply just because we are adults. To trust is natural. Trust describes healthy and fulfilling behavior. We have *learned* to hold back. We have *learned* to look for the negative signals. We have *learned* that many of the signals that emanate from the top are cloaked in double standards. We have *learned not* to trust.

This learned ***distrust*** often has valid roots. The British government's response to early unionization - transportation in chains to Australia[2] - is not easily purged from the psyche of those who follow. Hired to spy on, intimidate and even maim strikers, Henry Ford's "goons" left a heritage of fear, distrust and resentment that can be found in the beliefs that frame not a few of today's bargaining sessions. Even long after the events themselves are forgotten, the sense of being "wronged" can live on like a bad apple buried deep at the bottom of the barrel. It is a seed of discontent that has the capacity to destroy even the healthiest community. One need look no further than the Middle East, Bosnia or Northern Ireland for living examples.

It takes a lot of hard work to rebuild trust, to be a trustful employer. It starts with being ***absolutely consistent***. Consistency is found in:

- The ***story***. People do not forget, nor do they readily set aside past wrongs. We need a reason to let go of past prejudices; we need a reason to trust. And the reason had better be compelling! Organizations that build trust do so on the back of a compelling story. The employee's rationale is clear: I'll buy into a new way to do things, I will adopt a new attitude, only if what we are striving for is truly worthwhile...to me! As for consistency, it is not enough that a leader share the story; to make it live, to build trust, is to breath life into its realization every single day.

- The degree of ***stretch***. "Stretch" describes the spirit of learning, the freedom to act, and how the organization responds to those who fail to live up to agreed commitments.

  The lifeblood of any organization is how people learn. Learning is about challenging oneself against the best, investing in people, and taking time out for reflection. Learning is also about sharing. Organizations that lack a sense of community and/or fail to provide the tools of collaboration have little hope of ever reaping the benefits of trust.

  One of the learning success stories coming out of General Electric over the past two decades has been "workout." A collaborative workshop initially aimed at driving unnecessary cost out of the business, workout's secret is that it is a process based on trust. Leaders, when faced with suggested changes, are asked to start from the assumption that whatever the teams propose should, if possible, go ahead. As a result, the dialogue shifts from, "What's wrong with this proposal?" to, "What do we have to do to make this happen?" A mindset where *given the benefit of the doubt employees will get it right*, builds trust. By comparison, those who seek to control through criticism and/or are motivated by a "Gotcha!" mentality milk the organization of its essential vitality.

---

[2] The Tolpuddle martyrs: six English farm workers who, in the mid 1830s, were transported to Australia for forming a union.

No company can reach for greatness if it tolerates either (1) poor performers or (2) those who, even though they produce results, leave a trail of interpersonal debris. In either case failure to act makes the leader complicit in the employee's eventual and inevitable derailment. Failure to act also slowly but surely crushes the spirit of trust that must exist if the organization is to retain its high performers.

A century ago lack of trust meant that we created simple jobs supported by complex processes. The dilemma: bureaucracy slowly but surely sucks the life out of even the most creative of us. When the rules become more important than relationships, productivity is but the first casualty. Today no one joins an organization to stagnate, to become a cog in the machine, to park his or her brain in the parking lot when he/she arrives in the morning. No one wants to work for an organization devoid of trust. Change the assumptions about trust and we are quickly faced with the challenge of creating complex jobs and simple processes. The perfect antidote to bureaucracy is trust. Trust is a killer application that destroys hierarchy and strangles bosship. Trust naturally leads to freedom to act.

Freedom to act is but one quest in the search for the Grail of the modern organization: the advantage of size **combined with** an ethos that allows leaders to behave as if they were operating out of a small, agile, entrepreneurial business. Those striving to ascend to this organizational "nirvana" should keep in mind that risk and the courage to seize the moment do not readily thrive where strategy comes in a binder, and/or where the relationship between the center and its business operations can be characterized as one where the latter "need to ask permission." As ever…it's all about trust.

- The **speed** of response. Keep a customer waiting and the real cost isn't a missed order, it's a loss of trust. If an employee wants an answer to a personal issue, every additional day it takes to get back to him/her is a measure of how much trust needs to be rebuilt. When a successful candidate for a job is left waiting for an offer, every hour is an increment of trust shaved away. Positive feedback that does not follow the behavior in question is a trust-building opportunity missed. Perhaps even worse is dealing with one employee immediately while allowing others to languish in frustration, when the issues are perceived to be similar. Trust is in part about managing expectations. Just as there is a specific and implied promise, there is always a presumption about time. Meeting and/or beating that time expectation generates trust. Being tardy is to say, "I don't care." Trust-builders are deadline-busters.

> *Keep a customer waiting and the real cost isn't a missed order, it's a loss of trust.*

- How the organization *shares* information. People extend trust when they feel that they know what's going on. They draw their own conclusions when they are kept in the dark. If they find out what's going on from the local newspaper they are justifiably angry. Anger and trust are not comfortable bedfellows.

One of the enemies of trust is rumor. The cynics and the "told you so" merchants love rumor. It makes them feel important. It allows them to "spin" the rumor to meet their own selfish ends. The best way to feed rumor is to have executives make conflicting statements about the same topic. Even better: encourage executives to be critical of each other in public.

Open communication and a willingness to share absolutely as much as possible, as often as possible, nurtures trust. Organizations that do not have a website focusing on keeping employees up to date have, in essence, said to their workforce, "we've decided to delegate trust to a group of people we do not know and whose aims and interests are almost certainly not those of the business."

- The passion to *ship*. People want to work for an organization that has a quality product. People want to work for an organization that makes a contribution to society. People want to work for an organization that is positioned for tomorrow's success. Most of all though, people want to work for an organization that ships, that delivers on its promise to customers. People want to work for an organization that lives the brand. Nothing zaps the energy of an organization, nothing destroys trust faster than the belief that the product or service being produced delivers less than the customer has the right to demand. Trust cannot flourish if people don't care. Trust cannot live if people don't feel a sense of personal loss **when things go wrong!**

In the absence of trust one is left only with fear. The opposite of trust isn't distrust, it's small mindedness; a deepening of entitlement; games playing; and an endless, frenetic dash to mediocrity. A perfect petri dish for growing resentment and assumed wrong, fear is the companion of those who would eschew risk and the alter ego of those wedded to the status quo. Being a trustful employer isn't a philanthropic choice. Nor is it a fine weather activity. Leaders rebuild trust because without it leadership amounts to little more than a good suit, a nice briefcase and a decent haircut.

Trust and teamwork

The Twin Towers have fallen. But standing serene in New York Harbor is the Statue of Liberty, a symbol of hope. Leadership is about hope. The Lady in the harbor reminds us that leadership is about more than just change. It is, when everything else is stripped away, about enriching peoples' lives. What terrorism seeks to destroy is not merely freedom, but something perhaps even more precious…the belief in a better tomorrow.

The handmaiden of hope is trust. It is not enough to merely offer a richer sense of what is possible; people have to trust that it **will** happen. And when we face life's challenges most of us choose to do so not as an individual, but as part of *To share is the us in trust.* a group. It was ever thus. "The human ape," as Desmond Morris calls us, thrives exactly because when we work in a group, a "togetherness" lies within our grasp that, when realized, touches the very essence of who we are as a species.

At times of challenge we seek leadership. We need leadership. We are nurtured by the dream that is bigger than ourselves. Expansive dreams engage the spirit, and when we share that dream, we need someone who will champion our cause. In a world of turmoil we need someone who will help us pull the disparate pieces into a cohesive whole. In the face of criticism we seek someone who has the depth of character needed to act as a lightning rod and, in doing so, allow the work of the team to go on unimpeded. And at times of crisis we need a captain who affords the crew enough space to discover their own gift of greatness but who, at the same time, knows exactly when to step in and address that which isn't working.

And when we are called on to be that leader, trust – or the lack of it – will govern, to a large degree, that which is possible. It is a trust that is as fragile as the swallow's wing yet at the same time as buoyant as the currents that this tiny creature needs for its aerial acrobatics. To lead is to know how to instill trust. It is understanding that trust lies in never asking others to do what the leader him/herself is not prepared to do. It is knowing that the leader who lacks a passion for results will lose the goodwill of those who have it. It is measuring the team's success against both quantitative and qualitative goals. It is displaying tough empathy. It is using humor to defuse tension, and playfulness to facilitate team learning.

Archie Lee, the legendary marketing executive – "The Pause That Refreshes," Coca-Cola 1929 – preached that it isn't what a product is, but **what it does** that sells. It is not what trust is that matters, but **what trust does**. When team members trust each other they look each other full in the eye; they share information and ideas seamlessly both within and outside the team; they challenge each other as a natural extension of their own curiosity; they embrace difference and diversity as a means to enrich the team's potential for innovation; and they celebrate success with unbridled joy. To share is the *us* in trust.

Where trust is absent, stretch goals amount to little more than a negotiated compromise and risk becomes one more political factor to be weighed against self-interest and political expediency. As for mutual support, without trust, manipulative role-playing becomes the only game in town.

And what about trust in your own organization?

What are the organizational markers that the reader should note in evaluating the level of trust in his/her own organization? From the author's experience there are five key indicators:

1. *Rules.* It is something of a truism, but organizations with little trust love rules. They even love those rules that outlive the reason for their introduction in the first place. By comparison, employees that thrive in a spirit of trust do not hesitate when it comes to challenging rules that lack meaning, and are equally quick to ignore those which no longer make sense.

2. *Humor.* Organizations devoid of trust are sterile places to work. It takes trust to poke fun at institutional icons. Playfulness involves risk. Self-deprecative humor is a rite of passage that few embark on where making a mistake, being wrong, or not knowing, is a mark of failure.

3. *Transparency.* Trust can be seen in the comfort with which younger employees challenge senior executives. Trust is manifest in the openness and candor that punctuates meetings, presentations and training sessions. Trust is alive when those who don't live the values are confronted. Trust is found in the leader who shares his/her 360° feedback with the team. Trust thrives when those who coach are open to be coached. Trust moves to center stage when the CEO says, "I screwed up." Trust takes wing when respect for the individual is more important than respect for the position. Behavior to the contrary, lack of trust, a climate that embodies the philosophy of *know your place*, breeds a toxic climate that, like a harmful virus, first envelops and then destroys any healthy organizational tissue it comes into contact with.

4. *The quality and tone of the stories.* Organizations devoid of trust are communication factories that excel in the art of "why not." Trustful organizations produce just as many stories. The difference: the former repetitiously recount anecdotes anchored in the past, fueled by perceived wrong; the latter share stories that point the way to a richer future. One thrives on anger and frustration, the other on hope and possibility.

5. *The extent to which leaders feel compelled to follow the well-trodden path.* Organizations that lack trust, of necessity, need "sameness." A single mother should have no expectations of making it to the top flight; you have to be a technologist to run a technical business; proving oneself is a factor of time on the job; requests for capital have to be supported by a binder three inches thick; all expense accounts have to be reviewed by the boss before being paid; only officers of the company should be given a credit card; working from home means that people will goof off...all describe the path of least resistance. Trustful organizations deliberately seek

out the path of **greatest** resistance. They do so firstly because **they can**. They also do so because here lies latent possibility, here lies the root of innovation, here lies the source of breakthrough thinking, and here lies the capacity for reinvention.

*   *   *   *   *

In a world where leadership is far more about asking than telling, coaching, change, acting as a mentor, growth, connectability, collaboration, and a process way of working can only be understood if those involved realize that first and foremost…it's all about trust!

A number of writers have suggested that trust is like a bank account: you have to make regular deposits because it is inevitable there will be withdrawals. There is some truth in this, as anyone who has handled large-scale redundancies or a major merger will attest. What is missing from this picture is that visiting the bank, even on-line, is an activity we *fit into* our otherwise busy schedule. Trust isn't like a report or a presentation. It's not something we put into the planner and action when the time arrives. Trust is a characteristic of sustainability that successful leaders strive to win every single day. Trust and the implications for building trust are central to *everything* a leader does. Conversely, leaders who ignore trust are by omission creating the organizational equivalent of a black hole, a cultural void that will not only swallow up all of the resources within its orbit but, if not checked, prove impossible to escape. Anyone remember Enron?

At the center of Cosimo de' Medici's fifteenth century banking empire lay a simple issue. Without his reputation for honesty and straightforward dealing, the de' Medici fortune would never have been created and many of the great works of art that came out of Florence would never have been commissioned. If Ferdinand and Isabella had not trusted Columbus, the gold of the New World would not have made Spain the most powerful sixteenth-century nation in Europe. The building of the Great Transcontinental Railroad, the United Nations, the Internet, corporate governance, the fractured organization, a free market economy, democracy, the meaning of family…all were/are founded in no small measure on trust. No endeavor great or small can flourish without this ephemeral quality we call trust. *It's all about trust!*

What to do differently on Monday

1. Spend time listing and prioritizing your values. Is this the person that turns up for work every day or do you hide behind a mask that portrays who others want you to be? Be true to who you are. People want to know and will only truly trust the real you.

2. Allow yourself to challenge those things that you know to be wrong. To choose the safe and comfortable option is to walk the path of mediocrity. As a leader you **must** lead. Make your point known. Challenge. Learn to confront. Do so with respect, but also do so knowing that it takes courage to make a difference. Through our behavior we shape how others treat us. If we hold back, we tell others that it's okay for them to keep hidden that which we need to know.

3. List the five people in your business network who have the potential to make the greatest difference to your performance. Do the same thing for those who make a meaningful difference in your life generally. Describe both the agreed and the *implied* promises that shape each relationship. List the things you need to do to make every promise live. If there is any concern or doubt regarding the implied part of the promise, have a conversation with the individual in question and find out how you're doing.

4. Sweat the small stuff. Start and end meetings on time. Call back when you say you will. Be interrupted only when it is a genuine emergency. If you leave a message, give your number <u>twice</u> and state the time when you will be free. Be there. Get back to people fast. Meet every deadline. Even those issues that in the big picture appear to be of secondary importance matter deeply to someone.

5. Learn to listen…really listen! Be consistent. Admit when you're wrong. If you don't know, say so. Assume that given the chance people will get it right. Address poor performance. Build pride in the product. Break those rules you disagree with and in doing so give others permission to act in the same way. Enjoy your own sense of humor. Seek out the path of greatest resistance.

Chapter ten

The six paths to personal mastery

Book Three
Leadership of Self

---

*"If you limit your choices only to what seems possible
or reasonable, you disconnect yourself from what you
truly want, and all that is left is compromise."*

Robert Fritz

The quest for mastery

Striving for mastery is the embodiment of leadership of self. Mastery is about the stewardship of our own resources. Mastery is the very essence of being the very best that we can be. At some time in the near future each of us will face the reality that our three score and ten has run its course. Those who look back with pride will do so knowing that they reached for and touched their potential.

Mastery is the emotional genesis of any organization that wants to transcend the ordinary. For those with a passion to be the best, to be *the leader* is not enough. Mastery is about *leadership*. It is about example. It is about delivering with elegance and simplicity that which others find beyond their grasp. The Latin root of the word mastery is *magister* – the teacher. To be masterful is to teach.

One never truly reaches mastery; like life itself, it is an unfolding drama. Pablo Casals, the late, great cellist, was asked well into his eighties why he still practiced several hours a day. "Because I'm still getting better," he replied. Someone who claims to have *achieved* mastery is merely admitting that they have abandoned the dream.

The simplicity that communicates mastery is brought to life in the work of those who have reached the top of their profession. It can be observed in the newsreader whose delivery belies the fact that five minutes earlier the newsroom was a disaster area. It is manifest in the artistry of a Swedish glass blower. It has a home in the storytelling of the Australian aboriginee. It is evident in the art of the indigenous people of Northern Canada. In an organizational setting, it is found in the way a gifted communicator embraces the audience. It is central to the way that a masterful interviewer draws out information. It is contained in the way a top salesperson closes.

Mastery is apparent in the speed at which a challenge is accomplished. This takes us back to simplicity. Mastery distinguishes between that which is merely important and that which is absolutely essential. Mastery instinctively cuts to the heart of a problem. Mastery is the coach who hears not what is said, but what is meant. Mastery is the writer who in a few well-chosen lines can communicate what others fail to capture in several chapters.

Mastery has four stages. The first is *apprenticeship* – a time set aside to learn the basic tools of the trade. The quality of training provided at this highly impressionable stage of development has a lasting impact on the work ethic and standards of the performer.

The second is *learning how to perform*. For the mountaineer, it means honing his/her craft on the smaller peaks. For the actor, it amounts to accepting supporting roles in important plays. For the businessman or woman, it equates to those first tentative steps in managing a department, major account, or key project team.

The third stage of mastery is *reinvention*. Mastery cannot move forward until the individual is annealed by the heat of battle. Only then is he/she equipped to go beyond the established way. Only then can he/she make the work their own. For the actor, it is *his* Hamlet. For the concert pianist, it is her interpretation of Chopin. For the leader, it is turning around an ailing firm, bringing new life to an established enterprise, dealing with an organization in crisis.

The fourth stage of mastery is *serving*. Mastery in leadership is ultimately about what the leader contributes. It lies in the *giving* rather than the *taking*. In Chinese the word for mastery is made up of two syllables: "da" which describes greatness and "shi" which is to teach. To be "dashi" is to be no ordinary teacher, however. To be "dashi" is to teach with love.

Mastery is a passage that moves the learner through four distinct transformations. *Apprenticeship is of the head*. The young performer starts to *understand* the depth of his/her talent and, as a result, gets a sense of what is possible. It is where one's vision and goals move into focus.

Performing is of the hand. With his/her goals always in mind, the performer learns how to use the tools of the trade. The skills and competencies necessary for lasting success become anchored at a level of unconscious competency. The knowledge and skills needed to succeed become a natural part of how the performer thinks and acts.

Reinvention draws on the heart. The performer touches and understands his/her drive and desire. Those on a mastery track move from dependency to a sense of independence. Letting go comes from a compelling need to bridge the gap between the desired future state and the status quo. Excellence is driven, not by financial reward, but a passion for the "story." Steven Spielberg directed *The Color Purple* for $84,000.

Serving is of the spirit. It is about the joy of contribution and the riches that flow from interdependency. Leaders who don't give of their time in the growth of others are turning their back on mastery. Leaders who fail to see their role as one of service, regardless of their level in the organization, must be prepared to stand by while someone else conducts the master class.

To follow the path of mastery is to empower the head, enable the hand, engage the heart, and enrich the spirit.

Mastery is a river. Its flow is tentative and uncertain at its source, but as it moves closer to its delta it grows broader and deeper. Along the way each tributary represents an epiphany of awareness. The river eventually flows into the sea. To fuel nature's bounty, that same water evaporates and is cast down to the earth. Here it nourishes, yet again, the river's humble beginnings. Even the greatest performer exhibits a desire to return constantly to the wellspring of his/her talent, to be nurtured by the fundamental disciplines of his/her craft.

Learning during apprenticeship is modeled around instruction and the need for the aspirant to sit at the feet of the master. At this first stage of mastery the performer is acquiring the basic knowledge needed. Anchored in problems for which the performer must take ownership, the second stage of mastery develops essential "know-*how*." By "testing" him/herself, the performer is building emotional resilience, performance agility, and a rich understanding of the personal tools that constitute his/her personal make-up. Learning during the reinvention stage draws heavily on the extent to which the learner has the courage to keep pushing the boundaries. The final step in mastery speaks of, and brings, wisdom. At this stage of personal growth the critical skills and experience are already anchored. To be a "master" is to see new patterns and connections before anyone else. Mastery is evident in the act of creation.

The importance of a qualified instructor diminishes as the performer moves beyond his/her apprenticeship. When learning to perform, the player is significantly aided by access to a skilled and sensitive mentor. The mentor, in challenging the performer's assumptions, is enriching the learning experience. In sharing his/her own story he/she is helping the learner navigate through difficult rapids. When the learner starts to explore new possibilities, coaching comes to the fore. In the final stage of mastery the learner him/herself moves into the roles of instructor, coach, and mentor. This does not mean that "the master" turns his/her back on the opportunity to learn from others. Far from it; mastery cannot be developed in a vacuum. Mastery demands social awareness, rich feedback, and the ongoing input of respected collaborators.

The mastery journey is possible only where the learning involved is rooted in a rigorous adherence to discipline. Discipline is seen in the Zen archer's silent meditation before the release of the first arrow. Discipline rules the tenor's rehearsal. Discipline is apparent in the way a dancer prepares his/her body. Discipline is a habit that is so much a part of the leader's preparation that it is indistinguishable from the performance.

The six paths to mastery

The hurricane named "Change" is about to intensify. As if that were not problematic enough, the current maps chart a coastline that is no longer there and harbors that were once deemed "safe," can no longer be counted on. Any sane response makes nonsense of the view that leadership is the exclusive province of those who park in front of the building. To survive in a world where the whisper of global competition a decade ago has been transformed into a deafening crescendo, the organization must, of necessity, develop leaders at *every level* of the organization.

What sort of leader(s)? In a world where the competition never sleeps, the classic hero as leader, the lone performer whose success is based on going it alone, is best left to the imagination. The reality: no matter how well the man or woman at the top sings, today's music was written for a choir.

My work leads me to believe that there are six leadership roles pivotal to the success of the modern organization; six interlinked areas of organization performance; six distinct paths of mastery. *(See Figure ten.)* Look at an organization that has more stumbled its mumble than walked its talk, and it becomes quickly apparent that one or more of these critical areas of mastery have received scant attention. Examine an organization that has stubbed its toe as it attempted to step through the doorway marked *change*, and the evidence will be that

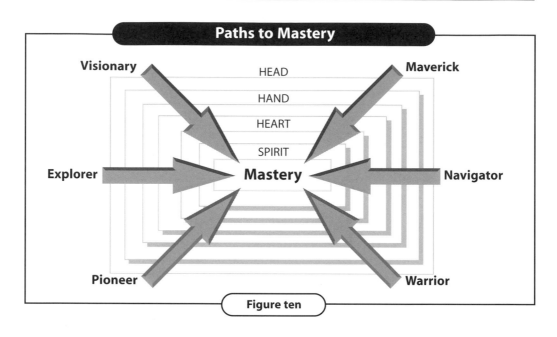

Paths to Mastery

Visionary — HEAD — Maverick
HAND
HEART
SPIRIT
Explorer — **Mastery** — Navigator
Pioneer — Warrior

Figure ten

even if the right music is playing, one or more of the leaders in question lacks the ability to reach the high notes.

For the reader, several questions should be to the fore as they explore each of the paths outlined.

1. What mastery path am I on? Am I following the right path?
   Does this path nurture and touch that which I am passionate about?

2. What stage of mastery have I achieved?
   What do I need to do to move further down my personal path of mastery?

3. What can the organization in which I play a leadership role do that it isn't doing now to engender mastery?

4. What can I personally do to support others in their quest for mastery?

What follows is a brief encounter with each path to mastery. What should not be forgotten is that each route to mastery, although drawn out of a different way to be, makes a vital contribution to the whole – where mastery is found wanting on one path (be it within the organization or within a key team) the potential contribution of **all** are diminished.

1. The Way of the Visionary

Considering the influence of the US in the second half of the twentieth century, there can be few men or women as successful in bringing about change as Martin Luther King, Jr.

If there was a defining moment for the American people in what was a period of dramatic social unrest it was King's "I Have a Dream" speech. On a fateful afternoon on August 28th 1963, his melodious voice rang out to the 200,000 civil rights marchers who stood before him. Millions more watched on the television. The speech, which lasted less than ten minutes, shook a nation to its very foundation.

His "dream" reached its vivid conclusion with the words of an old Negro spiritual: "Free at last! Free at last! Thank God Almighty, we are free at last." King's language changed not just a nation but the world – not with guns, not with violence, not with war, but with the power of a dream.

George Bush, Sr. called it the "vision thing." Others throw the term around with the abandon of a drunken sailor in his/her first port of call. The reality is, to be a visionary is to choose a path to mastery that is about creating the future. Without a vibrant, lucid, colorful, emotional and energizing sense of what tomorrow's success looks like, sounds like, and feels like, the change journey is over before it has begun.

To craft and communicate the vision is the unique role of the top executive, whether that is the CEO, the Divisional Director, the Country Manager, or the high-tech entrepreneur. To delegate the vision to another is akin to the Captain abandoning ship. A leader who lacks the creativity, spirit, judgment, flair, imagination and language necessary to craft a rich and meaningful vision is in the wrong role. To embark without a vision is to invite mutiny.

Some talk of a shared vision. There can be only one Captain, thus there can be only one vision. This does not mean that the vision should not be carefully weighed. The vessel's owners have a key role in formulating and validating the vision, and it is a poor Captain who does not know his/her crew. Ultimately, if those who are asked to buy in to the vision are not committed to the direction outlined, either those people need to be replaced or the vision is lacking.

Few organizations are led by a visionary. Oh, they have something called a vision, but throw it into a pile with those of the other companies in the industry and it is indistinguishable. What most organizations call a vision amounts to little more than a fleeting illusion of what can be. An even greater hurdle lies in the reality that for many who wear the Captain's stripes, the ability to craft a lucid vision demands mastery in language and story that lies outside their capability.

Does it matter that the man or woman at the helm is not a visionary? There is evidence in markets where the barriers to entry are high and where the competitive landscape is well established that organizations have been able to draw energy out of a vision created by the founder or past leader, even after his/her passing. There is truth in the notion that an organization with a strong brand is a little like an oil tanker: even if the engine stops it takes a long time to slow down. Without a vision, without a rich sense of tomorrow it is, nevertheless, slowing down! As we look forward it is difficult to imagine that tomorrow's organization will be afforded such luxury. When upstarts prove that virtually overnight they can redefine the way that an industry does business, even mega-giants have had to question the course they are on.

A vision doesn't live on paper. The notion of a vision statement is a contradiction in terms. Martin Luther King, Jr.'s words stirred a nation, not because of what was said, but because of how it was said and who said it. The vision has to live in people's hearts. That demands trust, respect, and the power of personal connection.

Without a compelling vision, opportunity is ill-defined. Without a vision there can be no emotional commitment to that being asked. Without an ability to create tomorrow in the hearts and minds of those who are asked to deliver, tomorrow is destined to remain a vague hope.

Visionaries succeed because they surface the dream that already lies within people's hearts.

The way of the visionary, however, is about far more than just writing the movie. The visionary's path is also that of producer, casting director, teambuilder, and host on the night the Oscars are handed out. And regardless of what the critics have to say, success is filling the theatre on a wet Monday evening in Liverpool. Wayne Gretzky's greatness was attributed to his ability to create a stream of mental images that allowed him to see not where the puck was, but where it was about to be. Were he not also masterful at putting the puck in the net, he would have remained an unknown player languishing in the minor leagues.

The way of the visionary is the most difficult of the master paths. The visionary successfully enters this path only after having gained a degree of mastery in one or, in rare exceptions, more than one of the other mastery disciplines, be it explorer, navigator, pioneer, warrior or even maverick. In accepting the conductor's baton the visionary is accepting that he/she can no longer be the first violinist.

It is true of all leadership but it is especially so of those on the path of the visionary: to lead is to serve. Meg Ryan said in a television interview that the most difficult thing to do as an actress was not to act. She added, perhaps even more poignantly, that the art in acting was to understand that acting wasn't about one's own role but about supporting the other players in their performance. Sir Adrian Cadbury, the former head of Cadbury Schweppes, once said: "Good leaders grow people, bad leaders stunt them; good leaders serve their followers, bad leaders enslave them." Visionaries succeed because they surface the dream that already lies within people's hearts.

2. The Way of the Explorer

Two passages in Stephen E. Ambrose's book *Undaunted Courage*, which describes Lewis and Clark's epic journey across the continental US, capture how the visionary and explorer paths differ. The first talks of Thomas Jefferson's ability to build the dream. "Beyond the fur trade and the other commerce, beyond the acquisition of knowledge, Jefferson and the subscribers wanted to tie the two coasts together, using the Missouri-Columbia water way to form the knot, in order to create a continent-wide empire for the United States. It was a breathtaking vision."[1] The way of the explorer is more pragmatic. "Lewis was deep into Indian country with only three men, and his main body three or four days' march away. He had a few geegaws as his currency. He had a frightened Indian reporting back to the Shoshones that strangers were in the area. He had just been through enough experiences for an entire expedition all in one day. He needed a good night's sleep, and lots of luck in the morning."[2]

Explorers live to stand on territory where no one else has set foot. Some explorers display an ability to see over the horizon, but many do not. The difference between the two paths lies in the time frame involved. A visionary creates a dream that often reaches far into the future. An explorer makes it pay!

Explorers are opportunists, they can smell the main chance. Many of those who write of the early mariners describe them as heroes, which indeed they were. What should not be forgotten is that Columbus and Drake and their kind were in it for the money! Hardship, deprivation, agony were all a price to be paid; they also represented an investment that had to yield an appropriate return.

Ben Rosen watched three Texas Instrument engineers sketch a design for a portable computer. Rosen bankrolled them. The outcome was a company that reached a billion dollars in sales faster than any company had in history. Its name: Compaq. One of those young engineers went by the name of Joseph R. "Rod" Canion. Canion, the visionary, was

[1] Page 71
[2] Page 267

made CEO.   Rosen, the explorer, knew exactly where his mastery lay – he went on to fund Lotus Development Corp.

In an organizational setting, explorers are out there every day in the marketplace.   They are highly attuned to the subtle shift, to nuances that others would miss.   The explorer goes and is accepted where others fear to tread.   While others wait for the fat lady to sing, the explorer is arranging to have drinks with her after the show.   And when others play tough, explorers buy up their gambling debts.

Explorers can take a path that leads them to be marketing executives or business development specialists.   Alternatively, they might just as easily focus on mergers and/or acquisitions or be the advertising guru who knows how to launch a brand.   It was called the Soundabout in the US, and the Freestyle in Sweden. It didn't sell. Marita, the man who built it, and Sony's engineering legend, overruled his marketing team and called it the Walkman.   The rest is history.   If the organization has to build a new plant in China and China is virgin turf, the organization needs an explorer. If you produce a Smart Car and it doesn't sell, send for an explorer.

Explorers are out there constantly testing the market place, their antenna always on the alert for the right signal.   Because of their strategic importance, the connection between explorers and the organization's visionary leader has to be very close.   When the name of the game is do or die growth, the top man or woman needs some degree of mastery in both.   Bill Gates seems to have added warrior to that list, although judging by his slow response to the Internet opportunity, and the antitrust issues that blindsided him, his level of mastery as a visionary seems questionable.

Explorers often don't fit easily into a corporate environment. In fact, they often behave badly when asked to remain in port for long stretches of time. Like the pioneers who are discussed later, explorers are happiest when they are out there battling the elements. Explorers differ from pioneers in one key respect: when an explorer gets involved, his/her impact is felt throughout the organization. Their mastery is apparent most readily, however, when faced with "the art of the deal." Or as Donald Trump says – "Go big or go home!" "The Donald" is the archetype explorer. He didn't invent Atlantic City, he just figured out how to make money there! An explorer's greatest joy is creating a new market, or going after the one acquisition that will propel the organization to greatness. And when faced with a choice, the explorer will always choose risk over comfort. When they do so, however, the impact of their ventures tends to be no small thing. Explorers play on the big table, and they play for high stakes. Cornelis de Houtman's voyage of discovery in 1595 embarked from Texel in Holland with four ships and 248 crewmembers. He returned on August 14th, 1597 with only eighty-nine men, seven of whom died shortly thereafter. There is another side to the story: Houtman's "success" gave birth to the Dutch East India Company, which in turn generated the wealth needed to sponsor some of the greatest works of art the world has ever known.

Explorers can be confused with warriors because they share many of their behavioral attributes. The difference in the paths they take is significant. When sales is on the agenda, explorers are the ones who negotiate for the city block, buy the most important house on it and then, when the competition is looking the other way, kick its front door down. Warriors run through the space created. Don King is an explorer. It takes a warrior to win in the ring, however. The explorer wants to change and control boxing. Oscar De La Hoya wants to destroy the opponent immediately in front of him.

Explorers have the courage, tenacity and personal ego needed to break the established patterns of play

Without explorers, the change process exists in a vacuum. All successful organizations have their explorers. Unfortunately, they are often forgotten in the change process, their insights spurned and their leadership role left unfulfilled, their work without linkage to the rest of those intimately involved in change. As a result the change agenda often lacks a true sense of the market place; processes are reengineered without a full appreciation of the next level of value proposition needed to succeed; and product is designed and built that should ideally be the province of a key supplier. Conversely, far too many deals are made and acquisitions pushed through without a full appreciation of the cultural implications involved.

Organizations need mastery in their key explorer roles. If mastery doesn't exist inside the business, a press-gang should go out and find the explorers it needs. Explorers have the courage, tenacity and personal ego needed to break the established patterns of play, to change mindsets, to smash presumed barriers. Without its explorers, tomorrow's organization will look much like today's. Without an explorer the ship is destined to rot in port, and even those that leave port end up either becalmed or worse, boarded by pirates. The 40% of companies that go missing from the Fortune 500 list every decade or so are those who haven't thought deeply enough about the explorer role; are those who have invested little in understanding the value of the explorer mastery path.

3. The Way of the Pioneer

One of the great scientific problems of the eighteenth century was longitude. Any sailor of the day worth his tot of rum could gauge latitude. All he had to do was gauge the height of the sun or, if it was night, a known star. Longitude was something else again. To understand longitude the Captain had to have a very accurate clock. To know his longitude at sea the

Captain needed to know both the time it was in his homeport and the time aboard ship. The problem: no such timepieces existed, with the result that many a mariner died of thirst when the port they were headed for failed to materialize.

To solve this problem the British Parliament, in the Longitude Act of 1714, offered a prize worth several million dollars in today's currency. Enter English clockmaker John Harrison, who against all odds, and despite having no formal education created, in the words of one historian,[3] "a series of virtually friction-free clocks that required no lubrication and no cleaning, that were made of materials impervious to rust, and that kept the moving parts perfectly balanced in relation to one another, regardless of how the world pitched or tossed them about."

Described as a "mechanic" by many of the other better-known contestants who did all they could to keep him from winning, Harrison's clock became a critical cog in the creation of the British Empire. It took him forty years, four decades of almost constant political intrigue orchestrated by some of the highest in the land but, in the end, Harrison took the prize.

Harrison was not a visionary, he lived to fulfill the dreams of others. He was not an explorer – he left that honor to the likes of Captain Cook. He was not personally a navigator, indeed he rarely went to sea. Harrison was a pioneer; he used his brilliant powers of innovation to exploit an opportunity that the visionaries, explorers, and navigators of the day had laid before him.

If explorers discover new lands, pioneers are the first to move in and exploit the opportunity. Every organization needs pioneers. Without pioneers even successful organizations are destined to be stuck in a world that is deemed comfortable and safe. Pioneers sally forth from the status quo not because they are told to do so, but because they simply enjoy being out there. They may complain that they are regularly shot at, stoned, and beaten up by the local population, but for them the joy of breaking new ground makes the hardships worthwhile.

Those on a pioneer path are found among the very best process engineers and within those who turn pure research into a product. A pioneer is any leader whose passion is to find a better and smarter way. Some of the best pioneers are those who call purchasing home but whose role is to find new suppliers and craft a better means to build value with those the organization already has. And the new plant in China – an explorer might build it but don't let him or her run it; that's the work of a pioneer. A visionary creates the dream. An explorer stakes out new territory. A navigator creates the charts that point the way forward. It is the pioneers and the warriors who exploit the opportunities presented.

---

[3] *Longitude* by David Sobel. Page 9.

What sustains the pioneer is a belief that land left barren, when approached in the right way, can become fertile soil that is ripe for the plough. To reap that harvest, pioneers are prepared to break trails that others would reject. To overcome the barriers that stand in their way, pioneers strip away hierarchy and empower people long before others see it as the right thing to do. Pioneers love to challenge ideas that have gone before. They explore new marketing channels even though they are told the technology isn't yet ready. They create products that the customer doesn't know it wants. They question *what is* just because it's there. Indeed, they become bored when ideas and break-through product ideas are not being pushed their way. Comfort and the idea of a roof over their head is a world to which many are wedded. Not so a pioneer. A pioneer's world comes alive when they are allowed to sleep under the stars; when they are given an opportunity to push a fully-laden wagon up an impossible incline; when they are asked to cross a river in flood; when they are told that something *can't be done*. Indeed, the way to inspire a pioneer is to say… "It can't be done."

Innovation and a passion to leap into new space are the very lifeblood of the pioneer.

Pioneers are important because they break new sod. By their actions they give permission for the more timid to act. Sometimes branded as dreamers and always mistrusted by the conservative and the conventional, pioneers not only enjoy working differently – they are compelled by their personality and overall make-up to seek new ways to tackle old problems. Innovation and a passion to leap into new space are the very lifeblood of the pioneer. For some, this means taking the high road and developing an ability to deal with unbelievable levels of complexity. For others, their "art" is to find a way to perform at a level of excellence with the absolute minimum level of resources.

Because they live in a world of innovation, pioneers stumble. As a result, even the most hardy understand that they are not perfect. The best pioneers deal with disappointment not through acceptance, but through a passionate desire to learn mixed with an appropriate degree of self-criticism and humor. Perhaps the most commanding quality of the best pioneers is that once they have an idea or a destination that they believe in, they don't quit – failure and/or disappointment only makes them want to succeed all the more.

Pioneers, once they halt their wagon, are readers. They are nurtured by the written word, they love to teach, and they truly excel when sharing their ideas with others. They study hard to understand the trails that are available, and take pride in knowing the route taken by others was one that they opened.

Not everyone is comfortable with pioneers and, indeed, they are open to criticism because their success invariably swings from the spectacular on one project to being trapped in a blind canyon on the next. As a result, their influence needs to be seen in terms of how they impact the total/future organization, not governed by a short-term punishment/reward mentality. Performance has to be seen in the long term and not limited by the quarterly review. Pioneering work has to be seen as an essential investment and not a cost. This does not mean that they can be given free rein regardless of the cost: each bridge, every river crossing, has its toll. Pioneers, when all is said and done, have to pay their way.

Organizations that do not recognize and embrace the value of those on a pioneer track destroy innovative zeal and with it the belief that it's okay to crayon outside the lines. An organization without space and support for its pioneers is not only a dull place to be, but one destined to find its warriors predictable and easy to ambush.

4. The Way of the Warrior

A British newspaper gave a rich description of a warrior's approach to life when quoting Arsène Wenger, the French manager of the English Premier League soccer club, Arsenal. "There is so much pressure from the group they will not tolerate anybody who does not have that fierce passion and mentality. You either show you are a winner or you are out. This is why, when I watch a player, I look at his body language. Individual character is more important than culture or nationality. Look at people like Emmanuel Petit or Tony Adams. Even if they won the World Cup, the European Cup and the Premiership in the same season, they would go on holiday and still want to win a five-a-side game on the beach. As long as there is a chance to win they will go for it."

An organization lives and dies by the passion and commitment of those who have chosen the way of the warrior.

An organization needs relatively few thought leaders. A world full of pioneers would be an exciting place to be but, as others have discovered, would be impossible to sustain. The warriors are those who create the value that allows thought leaders to build new dreams, and explorers the opportunity to live theirs. Without warriors the world is a dangerous place. Without warriors the organization cannot be sustained. An organization lives and dies by the passion and commitment of those who have chosen the way of the warrior.

Warriors are recognized by the weapons they carry and the paint that distinguishes their war party. Warriors are found in all parts of the enterprise, but in "best-in-class" organizations they are especially prolific in those parts of the organization generating revenue, producing product, and/or directly serving the customer.

Warriors are in the vanguard of change, not because it's the right or popular thing to do but because it means a better way to compete. For the same reason, warriors stamp on hierarchy and see unnecessary bureaucracy as a crime against mankind.

When the chase is on, warriors must be given the freedom to act. Important as they may be, dreams do not fill an empty belly. Warriors know this and, as a result, theirs is a world of action. The extraordinary is their benchmark, the impossible their goal. In the field they excel because they chase harder and hunt smarter than the competition. When it comes to production, their waking hours are dominated by a passion to reduce cost. When they serve the customer they do so as if their lives, not just their livelihood, depend upon it. To return empty-handed is the warrior's only fear.

Warriors love to hunt, but not alone. The war party, the team, is their unit of competitiveness. Warriors love to win. Moreover, they play to win not just for the rewards, but because they love the game. What drives warriors is the desire to compete at the highest level. To push and live at the edge is a natural and enriching part of their lives. They also love to celebrate the act of winning. What guides their actions is a shared set of values that determines what comes first. What binds them together is the belief that the whole is greater than the sum of the parts. What fuels their growth is a succinctly defined set of competencies reinforced and developed through open and honest feedback.

The very best warriors, the true warriors, have a gentle heart. For them, winning does not come at any price. Helping a fallen comrade, supporting a warrior new in the field, are reasons to give of their time. True warriors do not idly follow any leader. For them the "why" has to resonate in their heart. The reason for the battle has to speak to them deeply. As a result, when given the opportunity, warriors lead from the heart. They are nurtured, however, by the spirit. The challenge, the chase, the kill is not everything. They are ultimately driven by a respect for the foe, a love of their world, and a passion to serve.

When warrior language and aggression are used to describe the change journey but where the overall approach fails to encompass the warrior's heart and spirit, the outcome is likely to be not outstanding performance, but the unnecessary sacrifice of invaluable human capital. The way of the warrior lies not with unbridled aggression, fear, and malice, but with respect, self-sacrifice and willingness to share the hardship of combat.

In a world of constant and rapid change, warriors are a successful organization's true business strategists. Only those in the frontline, only those with an intimate involvement with the customer's emerging needs, can truly understand the forces that impact a dynamic marketplace.

This is not to say that those removed from the battle, those at the center, those in staff roles, do not have a dramatic role in the competitive arena. Their role is that of visionary, to explore, and to navigate. Their role is to aggressively challenge the mindset of those entrusted with the company's assets. Their role is to ensure that *their* warriors have the competency, character, commitment, and above all else the tools to win.

5. The Way of the Maverick

In 1965 Ralph Nader asked a simple question that rocked the American business establishment. In his book *Unsafe at Any Speed*, he asked why thousands of Americans were being killed or injured in automobile accidents when the technology existed to make the cars being built, far safer. Over vociferous objection from the industry his advocacy led to the passage of the 1966 National Traffic and Motor Vehicle Safety Act. It was legislation that led to the introduction of seat belts and air bags. Along the way his consumer activist group, the Center for Auto Safety, was responsible for the recall of the infamous Pinto with its exploding gas tank, the banning of the Firestone 500 tire for tread separation and the exposure of GM Firebomb pickups whose faulty fuel tanks burned to death hundreds of people. Meanwhile, Nader's financial resources amounted to less than half of what General Motors spent on a Superbowl commercial.

Mavericks often take up the mantle of being the company's collective conscience.

Nader didn't stop with the auto industry. He was instrumental in imposing federal standards on slaughterhouses, and his so-called "Nader's Raiders" brought about change in areas as diverse as baby food, insecticides, mercury poisoning, atomic energy, pension reform and coalmine safety. Nader's path to leadership is that of the maverick.

We all know those who have chosen the way of the maverick. We come across them in the form of a young idealistic trainee who has wonderful ideas and lets us know, regardless of his lack of experience, why he is right. We are listening to a maverick when the new recruit tells us with passion what's wrong with the company he/she has just joined. The research engineer who insists on doing it his/her own way is a maverick. And so is the sales person who harps on about what's wrong with the company's product offering. Mavericks come in all shapes and sizes.

Mavericks can be quiet and soft-spoken. That is until something comes up which does not mesh with their principles – and then they speak. Others are masters of dialogue and debate. Some are ignored when they interrupt the meeting yet one more time – but when something important comes up, surprisingly enough, they are listened to. Mavericks often take up the mantle of being the company's collective conscience. They are the first to say,

"I remember what happened the last time we did that!"

What do all these people have in common, and why do they represent a critical dimension of leadership? Leadership is about change. It is not about stability, it is about creating instability. It is not about comfort, it is about discomfort. Mavericks question the status quo. Mavericks push against the way things are. Mavericks want those around them to act and be different. Although they don't always do it in a positive or meaningful way, they are an essential source of tension and energy in the change process. The enemy of change isn't disagreement, it's apathy. It's not those who speak out we need to worry about, but those who keep their disagreement hidden. People who don't care, don't change. When all is said and done, mavericks care!

This doesn't mean that mavericks always listen, or that they are open to new ideas. What makes mavericks different is that they want to make a difference. The moaners, the groaners, the person who finds fault with everything – they aren't mavericks. The ever-present cynic isn't a maverick. Mavericks, in the way defined here, have ideas about not just what is wrong, but what should be done about it!

Mavericks stir up the water, they ask why, and who gains. Then they let you know who *they* think should gain! Mavericks, if they come on board, will do so with a passion. They seem to follow a path best described as "pendulum thinking." The more they are against it to begin with, the more they are for it when and if they do buy in.

Those following a maverick path often emerge as frontline thought leaders. They thrive in, and are drawn to this role, because they revel in conflict. They are somehow energized by it. Grass roots union leaders are a case in point. Representatives that follow the union "script" are, in a sense, easy to deal with because their concerns can be anticipated. Far more problematic is the shop steward who is a maverick even within his/her own ranks. Organizations need mavericks. Without them little is possible. With them nothing is impossible. They represent a source of leadership one way or another – either for or against. It is leadership that cannot be denied or ignored.

Mavericks can be difficult to manage. Some are simply a pain in the you-know-where. Others raise people's hackles not because they are abrasive, but because they are a distraction. They create value, however, the way a grain of sand in an oyster acts as a catalyst in the creation of a pearl. Their ability to create value in and of itself is often not great; it's the value that results from their "disruption" that makes a difference. This assumes, however, that the maverick is simply an individual with a point of view he/she "must" make. When the maverick in question brings mastery to his/her contribution, watch out – their ability to positively or negatively influence events is profound. Two names etched into the consciousness of the twentieth century embody the maverick: Gandhi and Nelson Mandela.

When change is on the agenda the lack of a maverick can have a lasting effect. John F. Kennedy believed he got pulled into the debacle known as the Bay of Pigs by what specialists in team process refer to as *group think*. It looked like a bold and plausible course of action, and because the President seemed to believe in it, everybody else went along. Later several members of Kennedy's Cabinet said they wished they had spoken up and made their concerns known. Kennedy's response was to appoint an individual at every Cabinet meeting thereafter who would play the role of maverick, someone who would present reasons why the idea being tabled should be rejected. And the person he appointed? The individual in attendance who was the one most knowledgeable on the topic.

6. The Way of the Navigator

On Wednesday April 10th, 1912 the world's largest ship slipped her berth. At 862 feet, more than 50,000 tons, and nine decks, she was more than a ship, she was a community afloat. The unique watertight compartments, the designers claimed, made her unsinkable.

But sink she did. Shortly after 11.30pm on Sunday April 14th, 1912 the Titanic, the greatest and most luxurious ship afloat, hit an iceberg.

The reasons for her descent to a watery grave two and a half miles below the surface have been a source of debate ever since. What is certain is that she was a vision of luxury that holds people spellbound to this day. In the form of Bruce Ismay, President of the White Star line, the Titanic's journey was made possible by an explorer, of sorts. Her designers – albeit flawed in their thinking about safety – were true pioneers. Warriors in the form of stokers were needed to shovel coal continuously into the giant boilers. Mavericks – well, they were finally heard from after the disaster.

Why did she sink? There are many reasons, but central to them all is that the course they steered put them in harm's way. The truth of the matter is that for the want of a navigator the ship was lost!

Navigators are a rare breed. Their role is to interpret the vision, listen to the explorers and map out the change journey. Without a "map" those who are being asked to follow are destined to be lost. Without a means to link strategy and action, the choice of sail is deferred to the one who shouts the loudest; the course ahead becomes the prerogative of the doubters and the malcontents.

A navigator is tough-minded. The navigator must challenge a vision that is ill or only partially formed. He/she must be prepared to do battle with the explorers if the intelligence is incomplete or the opportunity ill-defined. A navigator knows all the compass points, where the icebergs are, and if the channel is sandy, where the ship is most likely to run aground. And when the ship takes a course that he/she believes is wrong, staying silent is a hanging offence.

Navigators not only interpret the maps of others, they are charged with creating new and unique maps. This implies comfort with complexity, an ability to create language, expertise in communication, insight into structure, mastery of process, and an ability to orchestrate learning so that those who follow are equal to the task.

Failure to build mastery in the navigator role has brought about the early, and often unnecessary, demise of many organizations. Because their world moves so quickly, small high-tech/bio-tech start-ups were/are particularly susceptible to this malaise. Formed by a visionary, these aggressive young firms receive funding – less easily than in the past – because opportunity stares them in the face. As a result, they go out and hire their first group of warriors. By building on people they know, the founders tend to find an initial talent pool that is the right blend of enthusiasm and experience. If they are wise, they also set up a small team of pioneers to wrestle with tomorrow's offering. Early success, however, means that they have to quickly bring on board untried and inexperienced techno/bio-warriors. And it is here that things unravel. Complexity, a need to deliver that already promised, new competition which results in shorter lead times, a distorted vision, no shared language, confusion of roles, poor hiring practices, poor project management, lack of teamwork, misaligned compensation

> *Navigators not only interpret the maps of others, they are charged with creating new and unique maps.*

systems, little or no integration of new talent, anger, fear, disappointment – all shift attention and creative energy away from the customer toward an unhealthy focus on the internal politics of an organization that is, by now, "broken." High employee turnover and the cost of hiring yet more inexperienced warriors only makes the black hole the organization is falling into, deeper and blacker. Because by now the investors have a concern, the founders are told to hire a "professional manager." And so there arrives on the scene one who will introduce "controls." Controls are probably needed, but if the organization is not aided by someone who can chart an aggressive and comprehensive change map (navigator), then watch out for the rocks, because that is where the organization is headed.

To navigate means living in balance between the fastest course and the one that protects the ship. Because of the complexity of the role, the navigator often looks to others outside the organization to share their charts or even play a role in supporting the process of navigation.

The wise navigator seeks support, not from those who make the most colorful charts but from those who have themselves achieved a high level of mastery; mastery gained not from second hand accounts, but from many days spent at sea battling the elements.

A successful navigator must be not only the master of his/her craft, but someone who can guide the top team, rein in the pioneers, smooth out the rough edges of the warriors, deal with the excesses of the mavericks, and support building a culture that nurtures mastery. When anticipated landfall fails to appear on the horizon, or when high seas drive the ship off its course, it is to the navigator that those who doubt the wisdom of the course being charted will, in the first instance, turn. As a result, when the storm is raging the navigator is the one who will be expected to climb to the top of the tallest mast and survey the horizon – something that demands seamanship of the highest order.

The navigator needs to know how to use his/her elbows when, with the rest of the crew, he/she lines up for lunch. Indeed, a master navigator needs some of the qualities of a warrior. This does not mean that they approach the world in the same way. The difference is most apparent when it comes to the kill. The choice of weapon for the warrior is the cutlass – he/she likes to see the sight of blood. When the need arises, the navigator reaches for the rapier. The result is the same, but when a navigator puts someone to the sword even an expert pathologist may find it difficult to find an entry wound.

Master navigators are tough to find. Fortunate, indeed, is the organization that can look around its wheelhouse and identify a seasoned navigator. Navigators with savvy of foreign ports of call are rarer still. Traditionally, mastery in the navigator role is assumed to lie with the senior human resource professional in the organization. What is involved, however, implies far more than is traditionally encompassed by a senior "people role." Master navigators know the business context intimately, have a second sense as to where dangers lie, are the architects of change, create unique change tools and, as the need arises, are prepared to give even the Captain honest feedback.

Navigation is too important to be exclusively the prerogative of one individual or even one function. Few CEOs, for example, will make it through the raging storms that lie ahead if they do not possess a high degree of personal skill and aptitude in the art of navigation. This does not imply an absolute need for mastery. It does, however, mean knowing what they don't know and being smart enough to ask dumb questions. If, like Captain Smith, they fail to penetrate the mist of doubt that accompanies any dangerous journey, they are likely to find that they too are giving the order to abandon ship. Regardless of the nature of the journey, navigation is an issue that screams for collaboration – especially between the Captain and those that he/she calls on to deliver mastery at the top table.

An organization that wants for a master navigator finds it impossible to bridge the *thinking* organization with the *doing* organization. Without an experienced navigator the organization's change process is destined to be smashed on the rocks. Indeed, naïve are those who even contemplate leaving port without a master navigator on board.

Do Leaders Follow Only One Path?

Brian Moore, the Irish novelist, said that, "there comes a point in many people's lives when they can no longer play the role they have chosen for themselves. When that happens, we are like actors finding that someone has changed the play." Moore's quote leads one to ask, "Can, and indeed does, the leader need to reach for mastery along more than one path?" The question is not an easy one to answer, and perhaps the best response lies with the dollar-spinning rejoinder of that most savvy of life forms, the marketing consultant. It all depends!

Perhaps here it is worth stepping back and reiterating that the topic under review is not how to become the best flower arranger in the world or Europe's fastest typist – although both demand mastery. What we are profiling is **leadership** mastery. Leadership describes the qualities, attributes, and passion it takes to transform an organization (or part thereof) and, by implication, those in it. Moreover, we are not describing a leader who is merely good. Not even very good. Even the term "outstanding" doesn't do it. When we talk of mastery we are describing a leader who is knockdown, transformational, best I've ever seen, my god how did he/she do that, irreplaceable, state-of-the-art, I would love to work for him/her, sets the standards for the industry, do we ever need someone like that around here – good.

Mastery in more than one arena is not unknown. Churchill was a warrior, a visionary statesman, and when out of office, as those who faced the sting of his verbal pyrotechnics would attest, an absolutely masterful maverick. Peter Drucker, the famed management philosopher, is also considered to be one of the world's leading authorities on Japanese art (visionary and pioneer). Douglas MacArthur was clearly a masterful warrior. In helping Japan rise from the ashes after World War II, he also displayed mastery as a visionary.

That an organization needs mastery in the arenas outlined seems self-evident. Some might quibble with the terms used and the way each path to mastery has been described, but taken overall the proposed arenas of mastery ring true. The role of any team leader must, to some degree, encompass all six of the mastery paths described – even those in the middle of the organization have a critical visionary role. Equally important, a young man or woman striving to be all that they can be in a sales role isn't precluded from working to understand and develop expertise as a navigator. Expertise, however, should not be confused with mastery. Being damn good at something should not be confused with mastery. Mastery touches the core of our own greatness. It is about being immersed in one's passion and being the very best we can be. To be on a path to mastery is to be in flow. Queen Victoria was around when the point was first made: "Jack of all trades, master of none!" It is worth remembering that Walt Disney neither wrote, nor drew, the animated classics that bore his name. Thomas Edison, a pioneer extraordinaire, started dozens of companies almost all of which failed. At a more mundane level, Ray Kroc's attempts to add new dishes to McDonald's menu such as Kolacky, a Bohemian pastry, and Hula Burger, a sandwich featuring grilled pineapple and cheese – were all spectacularly unsuccessful.[4]

Savvy leaders, as they better understand where their mastery lies, move to an appropriate path. Authenticity, knowing our inner purpose, can only be realized if we are willing to go to the edge. True awareness and connection with *what is possible* remains a vague shadow of *what might be* for those who settle for a supporting role. To know ourselves we must move to center stage; we must be prepared to have the spotlight reveal our flaws. To reach new heights we must first go deep. To win we must be prepared to lose.

The differences are profound

The difference between each of the paths identified is far-reaching. The eagle (visionary) looks nothing like, nor acts in any way that would allow it to be confused with a Great Horned Owl (warrior). The former soars and rides on the air currents in order to identify distant opportunity. The latter – described by some experts as nature's best-equipped killing machine – can take prey three times its size, kill silently and instantly, and enjoy "lunch" while those around it are disabled by the total darkness.

The distinction can be seen in the "plumage." Don (the explorer) King's love me or leave me, bizarre, I just stuck my finger in an electric light socket, haircut says: "I'm me, I'm here, I'm having a good time, and I ain't leaving – so we just might as well do the deal." The scalp-hugging, drip-dry, razor (warrior) cut currently sported by some executives (worn slightly longer in women) by comparison, pronounces, "This hair stuff takes too much time, this is business, don't give me any grief!" Visionaries need expensive haircuts. Regardless who else is in the elevator, it is the visionary's right to stand in the center, so his/her hair has to look good from any angle. The more influential the navigator, the more distinguished they end up looking. Many navigators personify the "silver fox" look. Pioneers prefer an outdoors, log cabin, windswept, I don't care if the project is late, tomorrow we will be perfect, look. Mavericks don't worry too much about hair, they are much more concerned about which body part to get pierced next; they are much more interested in what will it take to provoke those in authority. A hat, of course, confuses everybody!

---

[4] Eric Schlosser. *Fast Food Nation: The Dark Side of the All-American Meal.* Page 33.

Those following different mastery paths learn differently. The visionary needs to be able to set the learning within the broader context. The explorer must be able to see and taste the value that will be the outcome of his/her investment. The navigator needs a map (conceptual model) of the territory that lies ahead. If one doesn't exist, the navigator will draw his/her own map. The scope and challenge of the problem motivates the pioneer. The warrior thrives when the competition is intense. The maverick disagrees, and then learns from the debate that ensues.

Conclusion

More often than not, leaders orchestrating major change stumble. The lack of success in integrating mergers and/or acquisitions is but one example of this malaise. The world that is unfolding before us suggests that the level of complexity and the scope of the new markets will only exacerbate the situation. What is already very difficult is about to get more so.

Assuming the above is true, we are faced with three distinct leadership challenges: (1) organizations are severely handicapped in the leadership of change if mastery in each of the six areas defined is not available; (2) leadership development that doesn't take into account all six mastery arenas is fundamentally flawed; and (3) leadership of self and mastery are indelibly linked. Pulling together a team at the top to drive change? Starting up a business? Frustrated by coaching those who are on the wrong path? Executive recruitment? Mentoring? Moving into a new role? The mastery implications for each are far-reaching.

Mastery means exploiting one's true potential. Sadly, modern society measures success not in terms of contribution, but in terms of positions and assumptions of power. We have been seduced into believing that mastery comes with a dollar sign attached. Each of us is born with an inner passion, a spark that, if ignited, will propel us into a rich future. It is an inherent sense of being that may mellow and reflect our personal growth and maturity, but it is never recast. There is a latent seed in all of us that flowers only if it is brought into the warmth and light of the sun. Following one's path to mastery entails being true to the purpose that lies within each of us. To touch mastery is to first find the way, to find one's true path. Only then can one stride boldly forth. Only then can each of us reap the harvest of our true potential. Only then can we become everything we are capable of being. **Leaders must lead.**

Things to do differently on Monday

1. Spend time thinking about your path to mastery. Is the work you are doing aligned with that path? If not, orchestrate the first steps to move to a path that builds on your unique capability. Think about the individual you report to, what path is he/she on? Does this insight provide an opportunity to change the way you communicate with him/her?

2. Does your team have access to all of the mastery paths described? Where the answer is no, seek out those who will make the team whole.

3. If accelerated change is on the agenda, does the team have access to a navigator? If not, find one. Without a navigator the probability of failure increases dramatically.

4. Make sure the talent acquisition process embraces team balance.

5. Take another look at those on your team who seem to be stuck. Is it an issue of capability or is he/she on the wrong path? Are there roles in the organization for which he/she is more suited? Act!

John O. Burdett is a widely respected international consultant focusing on what can best be described as "reinventing the leadership process."

John has a wealth of experience as a senior executive on both sides of the Atlantic. As a Consultant, he has worked in over thirty countries and for a wide range of organizations that are household names.

He holds a doctoral degree in Management Development and is a Fellow of the Chartered Institute of Personnel and Development.

A recipient of the prestigious "Trainer of the Year" by the Finnish Institute for International Trade, John received a teaching excellence award for his work on executive programs at University of Toronto. He has also taught on the executive MBA program at the Helsinki University of Technology.

John's previous book *New Role, New Reality* was nominated for Book of the Year by the US Society for Human Resource Management.